I0455432

Office of the
Comptroller of the Currency

Washington, DC 20219

Office *of the* Comptroller *of the* Currency

Director's Toolkit

THE ROLE
OF A NATIONAL
BANK DIRECTOR

THE
DIRECTOR'S
BOOK

October 2010

(reprint, September 2013)

THE ROLE
OF A NATIONAL
BANK DIRECTOR

THE

DIRECTOR'S
BOOK

Office of the Comptroller of the Currency

Washington, D.C.

PREFACE

A bank's board of directors plays a critical role in the successful operation of the bank. The health of a bank depends on a strong, independent, and attentive board that adopts effective corporate governance practices. The board has the fundamental responsibility of directing the management of the bank's business and affairs, and establishing a corporate culture that prevents the circumvention of safe and sound policies and procedures. In addition, directors have certain fiduciary responsibilities to the bank's shareholders, depositors, regulators, and communities it serves.

The Office of the Comptroller of the Currency (OCC), the agency responsible for regulating national banks,[1] recognizes the challenges facing current and prospective bank directors. The OCC published this book to help bank directors fulfill their duties in a prudent manner. The book summarizes laws and regulations that directors should be aware of and contains concepts and standards for the safe and sound operation of a bank.

The Director's Book was first published in 1987 and revised in 1997. This 2010 edition updates the guidance to reflect legal and regulatory changes since 1997. Directors should tailor their implementation of the guidance in this book to reflect the size, scope of operations, and risk profile of the bank on whose board they serve.

The guidance in this book does not constitute a legal opinion that conduct consistent with it protects a director from liability. Conversely, conduct inconsistent with such guidance does not necessarily result in violation of the law and possible liability. Instead, directors should

---

[1] The Dodd-Frank Wall Street Reform and Consumer Protection Act, signed into law on July 21, 2010, provides that supervisory authority for federal thrifts is to be transferred from the Office of Thrift Supervision to the OCC. The date of the transfer must be within one year of enactment, with the possibility of a six-month extension.

review their responsibilities and conduct on an ongoing basis and seek advice from counsel when necessary.

The guidance in this book does not create rights for banks or bank directors, or create obligations for the OCC. In particular, the OCC is not bound by any internal procedures set forth in the guidance, other than the extent to which the OCC may be bound by existing law.

Additional information on specific topics mentioned in this book can be found on the OCC's Web site at www.occ.treas.gov or on the OCC's National BankNet Web site at www.banknet.gov. National BankNet is an OCC-operated Web site exclusive for national banks. BankNet goes beyond standard Web-based services and enhances the private exchange of information between the OCC and the banks it charters. BankNet subscribers have access to numerous analytical tools that help directors compare a bank's performance with a custom peer group and established benchmarks.

TABLE OF CONTENTS

I

THE BOARD OF DIRECTORS

IMPORTANCE OF THE BOARD

National banks, like other corporate organizations, have shareholders who elect boards of directors. Bank directors face unique challenges, however, because banks differ from other corporations. Although banks, like other corporations, use their capital to support their activities, most of the funds banks put at risk belong to others, primarily depositors. Banks lend and invest customers' deposits to earn profits and reasonable returns to shareholders and to meet the credit needs of their communities. Generating a return to shareholders with depositors' funds requires that the board prudently consider the risks that a bank undertakes. Properly managing these risks is a critical challenge faced by the board and bank management.

Directors of a national bank are accountable not only to their shareholders and depositors but also to their regulators. Banks are regulated in part because Congress provides for federal insurance of deposits while also subjecting banks to regulatory oversight. This regulatory oversight is appropriate because of the risks inherent in the banking system, the safety net provided by deposit insurance, and the importance of a safe and sound banking system to the nation's economy.

The board sets the tone and direction of the bank and establishes guidelines on the nature and amount of risk the bank may take. The board oversees and supports management's efforts, reviews management's recommendations before approving or rejecting them, and makes sure that adequate controls and systems exist to identify and manage risks and address problems. The bank's systems and controls, as well as the volume and complexity of the controls, should be appropriate to the bank's size, the nature and scope of its operations, and its risk profile. The issues that the board faces are generally dictated by the nature and scope of the bank's operations. The size of the bank, however, does not necessarily mean that the bank does not offer sophisticated bank products. The board of a smaller bank may need to be as familiar with more sophisticated bank products as the board of a larger bank.

In difficult economic times or when management is ineffective, an active, involved board can help a bank survive. During these times, the board must evaluate the bank's problems, take appropriate corrective actions, and, when necessary, keep the bank operating until the board ensures that management is again effective and the bank's problems have been resolved.

A board should perform a self-assessment of its effectiveness periodically and determine whether it is taking the steps necessary to correct deficiencies. It also should review how well board committees are meeting their responsibilities. Bank counsel, auditors, or other advisors can often assist the board in these efforts. OCC examiners evaluate how well the board meets its responsibilities and make recommendations for improvement if they find weaknesses.

A board should conduct orientation programs for new directors. While these programs vary based on the bank's size and complexity, at a minimum these programs should explain the operation of the bank and the banking industry and clearly outline the responsibilities of board members, individually and as a group. Ongoing education programs that describe local and overall economic conditions, emerging industry developments, opportunities, and risks also are important tools for maintaining director expertise and board effectiveness.

BOARD COMPOSITION

A board's effectiveness depends in large part on how well its members work together to identify and address issues important to the bank's future. A national bank must have at least five, but no more than 25, directors. The board and shareholders establish the number of directors in the bank's bylaws.

Membership on a bank's board gives a person a valuable opportunity to share his or her expertise with the bank, help the community, and advance professionally. The position of director is prestigious, identifying the incumbents as trusted and respected members of the communities in which the bank operates. At the same time, a well-respected individual's alliance with a bank may lend stature to the bank. Board membership is also an opportunity to contribute to the local economy's growth and development.

Typically, a board includes individuals who are bank officers or employees—called "management" or "inside" directors—and "outside" directors who are neither officers nor employees of the bank. Outside, independent[2] directors bring experiences from their fields of expertise. These experiences provide perspective and objectivity as the director oversees bank operations and evaluates management recommendations.

When searching for new directors, boards should seek individuals who exercise independent judgment and who actively participate in decision making. The principal qualities of an effective bank director include strength of character, an inquiring and independent mind, practical wisdom, and sound judgment. Some boards establish additional criteria to supplement these attributes. These may include individual qualifications, such as technical skills, career specialization, or specific backgrounds. Such criteria may change over time if, for example,

---

[2] Generally, a director is viewed as independent if he or she is a non-management director free of any family relationship or any material business or professional relationship (other than stock ownership and the directorship itself) with the bank or its management. Additional requirements for meeting the independence standard are required by the Sarbanes-Oxley Act for public banking companies and by 12 CFR 363 for larger banking companies.

the bank plans to offer new products or services or expand beyond current markets.

The board's nominating procedures can help identify and retain qualified directors. Many banks nominate directors on the basis of their independence, diversity, technical qualifications, and capabilities. Many directors are also selected because of their position in the community or their relationship to the bank (for example, a large shareholder).

Prospective directors should determine whether the bank's board actively oversees bank operations. If directors, outside directors in particular, are not encouraged to actively contribute and participate in board discussions, prospective directors should weigh this carefully against their impending responsibilities and corresponding potential liabilities when deciding whether to serve.

In most cases, individuals nominated as national bank directors serve in that capacity immediately after they are approved in accordance with the bylaws. If, however, the bank is not in compliance with minimum capital requirements, is in a troubled condition, or is not in compliance with a directive to correct a problem promptly, the bank must file a notice with the OCC about proposed new directors before they can serve on the board. The OCC also may object to proposed directors of new banks during the first two years the bank is in business.

When prior notice is required, the OCC conducts background checks and reviews the biographical and financial information submitted by the proposed director. The OCC has 90 days to disapprove the nomination of a proposed director.

In addition to the citizenship and residency requirements contained in 12 USC 72, the qualifications of a candidate seeking to become a member of the board of directors of a national bank include

☐ Basic knowledge of the banking industry, the financial regulatory system, and the laws and regulations that govern the operation of the institution.

- Willingness to put the interests of the bank ahead of personal interests.

- Willingness to avoid conflicts of interests.

- Knowledge of the communities served by the bank.

- Background, knowledge, and experience in business or another discipline to facilitate oversight of the bank.

- Willingness and ability to commit the time necessary to prepare for and regularly attend board and committee meetings.

ADVISORY DIRECTORS

Some institutions supplement their boards with advisory directors, with titles such as associate directors, honorary directors, or directors emeriti. Advisory directors may serve the board, directly or indirectly, through an advisory board. These individuals provide information and advice but do not vote as part of the board.

A board with advisory directors generally brings a broader perspective to a bank. Advisory directors are often former directors of newly purchased banks and may represent a large constituency of customers or communities that are not otherwise represented on the board. A bank may use advisory directors in the following situations:

- When the operations of the bank are geographically dispersed and the board wants input from more segments of the communities served by the bank.

- When the board itself is small and the directors want direct involvement with a broader array of community leaders.

- To assist in business development.

- To gain access to special expertise to assist the board in its planning and decision-making activities.

- To help identify likely candidates for future board openings.

Because of their limited role, advisory directors generally are not liable for board decisions. The facts and circumstances of a particular situation, however, as well as whether an advisory director functions in effect as a full director, are likely to determine whether an advisory director may have liability for individual decisions, including factors such as

☐ Whether advisory directors were elected or appointed.

☐ How advisory directors are identified in corporate documents.

☐ How advisory directors participated in board meetings.

☐ Whether advisory directors exercised significant influence on the voting process.

☐ How advisory directors were compensated for attending board meetings.

☐ Whether the advisory director had a prior relationship with the bank.

An advisory director who in fact functions as a full director may be liable for board decisions in which he or she participated as if that person were a full director. Individuals cannot shield their actions from liability simply by inserting the word "advisory" in their title.

THE BOARD AND THE OCC

SUPERVISORY ACTIVITIES

The OCC supervises national banks by conducting on-site examinations and by performing periodic monitoring. These activities help determine the condition of individual banks and the overall stability of the national banking system. The OCC and other federal bank regulatory agencies use the Uniform Financial Institutions Rating System, or "CAMELS," to assign composite and component ratings to banks.[3] The frequency of OCC on-site examinations is determined by the bank's size, complexity, risk profile, and condition. These on-site examinations are conducted either annually or up to every 18 months (unless the bank is experiencing problems, in which case it may be examined more frequently).

---

[3] A bank's composite CAMELS rating integrates ratings from six component areas—capital adequacy, asset quality, management, earnings, liquidity, and sensitivity to market risk. The ratings range from 1 to 5 with 1 being the highest rating and least supervisory concern.

Examiners meet with bank management during the examination to obtain information or to discuss issues. When the examination is complete, the examiners prepare a report of examination and conduct a meeting with the bank's board of directors (except for some smaller affiliates of large banks, in which case the meeting may be conducted with the lead bank's board) to discuss the results of the examination. Each director is responsible for thoroughly reviewing and signing the report of examination.

An environment in which examiners and board members openly and honestly communicate benefits a bank. OCC examiners have experience with a broad range of banking activities and can provide independent, objective advice on safe and sound banking principles and compliance with laws and regulations.

Directors are encouraged to meet with OCC examiners to discuss the condition of the bank and the results of the examination. Outside directors may choose to meet with OCC examiners without management's presence. Directors should pay close attention to and review carefully any written communications from the OCC. They should ask questions and raise issues of concern. Directors also should ensure that bank management completes any specific follow-up actions in a timely manner.

The activities of OCC examiners do not diminish the board's responsibilities to oversee the management and operation of the bank. Directors are independently responsible for knowing the condition of the bank and should not rely on the examiners as their sole source of information to identify or correct problems. Instead, the board should look to its senior management, its auditors, and other outside experts to identify and correct any problems.

APPEALS PROCESS

The OCC desires consistent and equitable supervision and seeks to resolve disputes that arise during the supervisory process fairly and expeditiously in an informal, professional manner. When disputes cannot be resolved informally, the board of directors of a national bank may ask its supervisory office to review the disputed matter or appeal the matter to the OCC Ombudsman.

Functioning as an independent adviser and decision maker, the OCC ombudsman can accept appeals from boards of directors related to, for example, examination ratings, the adequacy of loan loss reserve positions, and significant loan classifications. The ombudsman may not accept appeals related to the appointment of receivers and conservators, preliminary examination conclusions communicated to a national bank before a final report of examination is issued, enforcement-related actions or decisions, formal and informal rulemakings pursuant to the Administrative Procedures Act, or requests for information filed under the Freedom of Information Act. With the prior consent of the Comptroller of the Currency, the ombudsman may stay an appealable agency decision or action during the resolution of an appealable matter.

COMPLIANCE WITH LAWS AND REGULATIONS

A board of directors should be aware that, in addition to the OCC's supervisory responsibilities, the agency enforces banking and other laws and regulations that apply to national banks. For example, the OCC enforces compliance with the legal lending limit, which restricts the amount a bank may lend to a single borrower (or to related borrowers that are financially interdependent) to prevent undue concentrations of credit. Other banking laws the OCC enforces include restrictions on loans to insiders and transactions with affiliates. Insider and affiliate transaction laws are intended to prevent the misuse of a bank's resources by such persons or companies.

Other laws and regulations under OCC purview include those designed to protect consumers[4] or to facilitate broader law enforcement efforts. For example, the OCC administers compliance with the Equal Credit Opportunity Act, a law that requires lenders to make credit decisions without discriminating on the basis of certain enumerated factors. The OCC's law enforcement efforts include examining for, and enforcing compliance with, the Bank Secrecy Act (BSA), Anti-Money Laundering program requirements, and Office of Foreign Assets Control regulations. The OCC also assesses a bank's performance under the Community Reinvestment Act (CRA).

REGULATION OF PROBLEM BANKS

Problem banks generally have composite CAMELS ratings of 3, 4, or 5 and often possess one or more of the following deficiencies:

- ☐ Excessive growth or aggressive growth strategies.

- ☐ Ineffective or dishonest management.

- ☐ Insider abuse and fraud.

- ☐ Excessive amount of low-quality assets or inordinate concentrations of credit.

- ☐ Insufficient capital.

- ☐ Inadequate policies, procedures, or internal controls.

- ☐ Deferred loan loss provisions, chargeoffs, or recognition of securities impairment.

- ☐ Strained liquidity, including reliance on brokered deposits.

- ☐ Significant medium- and long-term interest rate risk exposure.

- ☐ Lack of a viable strategic plan.

- ☐ Failure of the board or senior management to understand the bank's activities and their risks.

---

[4] Under the Dodd-Frank Wall Street Reform and Consumer Protection Act, effective July 21, 2011, the Bureau of Consumer Financial Protection will assume certain designated consumer financial protection functions of the OCC for banks with more than $10 billion in assets.

When the OCC identifies or communicates problems or weaknesses to a bank, the bank's senior management and board of directors are expected to promptly correct them. The actions the bank takes or agrees to take in response to problems or weaknesses are important factors in determining whether the OCC takes enforcement action and the severity of that action. If the OCC believes a bank has significant weaknesses, the OCC may conclude that the bank requires additional or special supervision. In such cases, the OCC usually examines and monitors the bank more frequently. The OCC works with the board and bank management to determine necessary corrective action to return the bank to a safe and sound condition.

A problem bank becomes subject to a number of enhanced regulatory restrictions as its composite or component CAMELS ratings or Prompt Corrective Action capital category declines or when it is subject to a formal enforcement action. The board is responsible for ensuring that bank management is aware of such restrictions and complies with them.

THE BOARD'S ROLE IN RISK MANAGEMENT

The OCC recognizes that banking is a business of assuming risks in order to earn profits. Risk levels, however, must be appropriately managed. A bank's safety and soundness are contingent upon effectively managing its risk exposures. Some transactions or activities may expose a particular bank to a level of risk so great that its board may reasonably conclude that no amount of sound risk management can effectively control it.

To manage risk effectively, a bank must have a well-informed board of directors that guides its strategic direction. A key component of strategic direction is establishing the bank's risk tolerance. The board establishes the bank's risk tolerance by approving policies that set standards for the nature and level of risk the bank is willing to assume. These policies should generally be written and periodically reviewed and updated.

After adopting policies, the board must ensure that its guidance is effectively communicated and adhered to throughout the bank. A well-designed monitoring system is the best way for the board to hold management accountable for operating within established risk tolerance levels.

Capable management and appropriate staffing are essential to effective risk management. Bank management is responsible for the implementation, integrity, and maintenance of risk management systems. Management must

☐ Keep the directors adequately informed about the bank's activities.

☐ Implement the board-approved strategic direction.

☐ Develop policies that reflect the bank's risk tolerance and that are compatible with the bank's strategic direction.

☐ Oversee the development and maintenance of management information systems that provide timely, accurate, and pertinent information.

☐ Ensure that the strategic direction and risk tolerances are effectively communicated and adhered to throughout the organization.

Because market conditions and bank structures vary, no single risk management system works for all banks. Each bank should develop its own risk management system tailored to its needs and circumstances. The sophistication of the risk management system increases with the size, complexity, and geographic diversity of each bank. All sound risk management systems, however, have several common fundamentals. For example, bank staff responsible for implementing sound risk management systems should perform those duties independently of the bank's risk-taking activities. Regardless of the risk management system's design, it should include mechanisms for identifying, measuring, monitoring, and controlling risks:

☐ **Identifying.** Proper risk identification focuses on recognizing and understanding existing risks or risks that may arise from changing economic conditions or new business initiatives. Risk identification should be a continuous process, and risks should be understood at both the transaction (individual) and portfolio (aggregate) level. As part of its identification process, banks should consider not only the risks arising from normal or "business as usual" conditions, but also the nature and level of risks that may arise from more adverse or "stressed" conditions.

☐ **Measuring.** Accurate and timely measurement of risk is essential to effective risk management systems. A bank that does not have risk measurement tools has limited ability to control or monitor risk levels. The sophistication of the risk measurement tools a bank uses should reflect the type and complexity of its products and services. All banks should periodically test their measurement tools to make sure they are accurate. Sound risk measurement tools assess the risks at the transaction and portfolio levels.

☐ **Monitoring.** The bank should monitor risk levels to ensure timely review of risk positions and exceptions. Monitoring reports should be timely, accurate, and informative, and should be distributed to appropriate individuals for action, when needed.

☐ **Controlling.** The bank should establish and communicate risk limits through policies, standards, and procedures that define responsibility and authority. These limits should serve as a means to control exposures to the various risks associated with the bank's activities. The limits should be tools that management can adjust when conditions or risk tolerances change. The bank should have a process to authorize and document exceptions or changes to risk limits when they are warranted.

OCC'S SUPERVISION BY RISK PROGRAM

This overview of the OCC's supervision by risk program is included to provide boards of directors with a general description of the importance of risk management to banking. More detail on the supervision by risk program can be found in the "Bank Supervision Process" booklet of the *Comptroller's Handbook.*

The OCC's supervision of national banks is directed at identifying significant or emerging problems in individual banks and the banking system and ensuring that such problems are appropriately corrected. Because banking is essentially a business of assuming and managing risk, the OCC has adopted a supervisory philosophy that is centered on evaluating risks and risk management systems. The OCC applies this philosophy to all supervisory activities it conducts, including safety and soundness, information technology, compliance, and fiduciary activities.

Supervision by risk consists of determining the quantity of risk exposure in a bank and evaluating the quality of risk management systems in place to control risk. Supervision by risk provides consistent definitions of risk, a structure for assessing these risks, and integration of risk assessment in the supervisory process.

Supervision by risk places the responsibility for controlling risks with the board of directors and management. The OCC assesses how well a bank manages its risks over time, rather than assessing only the condition at a single point in time.

CATEGORIES OF RISK

Risk is the potential that events, expected or unanticipated, may have an adverse effect on a bank's earnings, capital, or enterprise value. To achieve more comprehensive and efficient examinations of national banks, the OCC has defined eight categories of risk inherent in bank activities. These risks may be both current and prospective and are not mutually exclusive, because any product or service may expose a bank to multiple risks. The risks may also be interdependent—an increase in one category may cause an increase in others. For analysis and discussion purposes, however, the OCC identifies and assesses the risks separately.

The following is a brief description of the eight risks. A more complete discussion of these risks is contained in the "Community Bank Supervision" and "Large Bank Supervision" booklets of the *Comptroller's Handbook*. The OCC does not require banks to adopt its risk definitions. Directors and bank management should, however, understand the nature of these risks and ensure that the bank's risk management systems adequately address all relevant risks.

☐ **Credit risk.** The risk to earnings or capital arising from an obligor's failure to meet the terms of any contract with the bank or otherwise to perform as agreed. Credit risk is found in all activities where success depends on counterparty, issuer, or borrower performance. It arises any time bank funds are extended, committed, invested, or otherwise exposed through actual or implied contractual agreements, whether reflected on or off the balance sheet.

☐ **Interest rate risk.** The risk to earnings or capital arising from movements in interest rates. Interest rate risk arises from differences between the timing of rate changes and the timing of cash flows (repricing risk), from changing rate relationships among different yield curves affecting bank activities (basis risk), from changing rate relationships across the spectrum of maturities (yield curve risk), and from interest-related options embedded in bank products (options risk).

☐ **Liquidity risk.** The risk to earnings or capital arising from a bank's inability to meet its obligations when they come due without incurring unacceptable losses. Liquidity risk includes the inability to manage unplanned decreases or changes in funding sources. Liquidity risk also arises from the failure to recognize or address changes in market conditions that affect the ability to liquidate assets quickly and with minimal loss in value.

☐ **Price risk.** The risk to earnings or capital arising from changes in the value of either trading portfolios or other obligations that are entered into as part of distributing risk. These portfolios are typically subject to daily price movements and are accounted for primarily on a mark-to-market basis. This risk arises most significantly from market-making, dealing, and position-taking in interest rate, foreign exchange, equity, commodities, and credit markets. Price risk also arises in banking activities whose value changes are reflected in the income statement, such as in lending pipelines and mortgage servicing rights. The risk to earnings or capital arising from the conversion of a bank's financial statements from foreign currency translation is also price risk.

☐ **Operational risk.** The risk to earnings or capital arising from inadequate or failed internal processes or systems, the misconduct or errors of people, and adverse external events. Operational losses result from internal fraud; external fraud; employment practices and workplace safety; clients, products, and business practices;

damage to physical assets; business disruption and systems failures; and execution, delivery, and process management.

☐ **Compliance risk.** The risk to earnings or capital arising from violations of, or nonconformance with, laws, rules, regulations, prescribed practices, internal policies and procedures, or ethical standards. Compliance risk also arises in situations where the laws or rules governing certain bank products or activities of the bank's clients may be ambiguous or untested. This risk exposes the bank to fines, civil money penalties, payment of damages, and the voiding of contracts. Compliance risk can lead to diminished reputation, reduced enterprise value, limited business opportunities, reduced expansion potential, and an inability to enforce contracts.

☐ **Strategic risk.** The risk to earnings, capital, or enterprise value arising from adverse business decisions, improper implementation of decisions, or lack of responsiveness to industry changes. This risk is a function of the compatibility of an organization's strategic goals, the business strategies developed to achieve those goals, the resources deployed, and the quality of implementation. The resources needed to carry out business strategies are both tangible and intangible. They include communication channels, operating systems, delivery networks, and managerial capacities and capabilities. The organization's internal characteristics must be evaluated against the effect of economic, technological, competitive, regulatory, and other environmental changes.

☐ **Reputation risk.** The risk to earnings, capital, or enterprise value arising from negative public opinion. This risk affects the bank's ability to establish new relationships or services or continue servicing existing relationships. This risk may expose the bank to litigation or financial loss, or impair its competitiveness or ability to attract or retain funding or capital. Reputation risk exposure is present throughout the bank and requires management to exercise an abundance of caution in dealing with customers, investors, and the community.

The board should ensure that bank management adequately identifies the risks associated with particular activities and has put in place systems and controls to manage those risks. When OCC examiners assess a bank's risk management system, they consider policies, processes, personnel, and control systems. A significant deficiency in one or more of these components constitutes a deficiency in risk management. All of these components are important, but the sophistication of each may vary depending on the bank's complexity. Noncomplex community banks normally have less formalized policies, processes, and control systems in place than do large or more complex banks.

☐ **Policies** are written or verbal statements of the bank's commitment to pursue certain results. They set standards and courses of action to achieve specific objectives established by the board. Policies should be consistent with the bank's underlying mission, values, and principles. They also clarify the bank's tolerance for risk. Mechanisms should be in place to trigger a review of policies in the event that activities or objectives change.

☐ **Processes** are the procedures, programs, and practices that impose order on the bank's pursuit of its objectives. Processes define how daily activities are carried out. Effective processes are consistent with the underlying policies and are governed by appropriate checks and balances.

☐ **Personnel** are the bank staff and managers who execute or oversee processes. Personnel should be qualified and competent and should perform as expected. They should understand the bank's mission, values, policies, and processes. Compensation programs should be designed to attract, develop, and retain qualified personnel and encourage strong risk management practices that appropriately balance risk and reward.

☐ **Control systems** are the tools and information systems that bank managers use to measure performance, make decisions about risk, and assess the effectiveness of processes. The audit program is a critical element of the bank's control systems. Feedback from these tools and information systems must be timely, accurate, and pertinent.

When risks are excessive or not properly managed, the OCC works with the board and bank management to determine necessary corrective action.

THE BOARD AND OTHER REGULATORS

The boards of directors of national banks may have occasion to contact federal bank regulatory agencies other than the OCC, namely, the Board of Governors of the Federal Reserve System and the Federal Deposit Insurance Corporation (FDIC). The following table summarizes the primary and secondary supervisory responsibilities of the three bank regulatory agencies. The table also shows that these agencies have jurisdictions that sometimes overlap. When this occurs, the agencies work together and share information to reduce burden to both the bank and the agencies.

Bank Regulatory Agency	Supervisory Responsibility[a]
OCC	National Banks (Primary) Federal Branches and Agencies of Foreign Banks (Primary)
Board of Governors of the Federal Reserve System	Bank Holding Companies (Primary) State Member Banks (Primary) National Banks (Secondary) Federal Branches and Agencies of Foreign Banks (Secondary)
FDIC	Insured State Nonmember Banks (Primary) Insured National Banks (Secondary) Insured State Member Banks (Secondary) Insured Branches and Agencies of Foreign Banks (Secondary)

[a] The Dodd-Frank Wall Street Reform and Consumer Protection Act, signed into law on July 21, 2010, provides that supervisory authority for federal thrifts, state thrifts, and thrift holding companies is to be transferred from the Office of Thrift Supervision to the OCC, FDIC, and Federal Reserve, respectively. The date of the transfer must be within one year of enactment, with the possibility of a six-month extension.

Bank boards also should be aware that certain activities may be subject to regulation by other entities.[5] The Gramm-Leach-Bliley Act codified the concept of "functional regulation," recognizing the role of the state insurance commissioners, the U.S. Securities and Exchange Commission (SEC), and the U.S. Commodities Futures Trading Commission as the primary regulators of insurance, securities, and commodities activities, respectively.

---

[5] See footnote 4.

II

THE BOARD'S RESPONSIBILITIES

ESTABLISH AN APPROPRIATE CORPORATE CULTURE

HIRE AND RETAIN COMPETENT MANAGEMENT

BE AWARE OF THE BANK'S OPERATING ENVIRONMENT

MAINTAIN AN APPROPRIATE BOARD STRUCTURE

MONITOR OPERATIONS

OVERSEE BUSINESS PERFORMANCE

SERVE COMMUNITY CREDIT NEEDS

Although a board of directors does not guarantee a bank's success, the board must oversee the bank to ensure that the bank operates in a safe and sound manner and complies with applicable laws and regulations. The board must establish an appropriate corporate culture and set the "tone at the top," hire and retain competent management, stay informed about the bank's operating environment, and ensure that the bank has a risk management system suitable for the bank's size and activities. The board also must oversee the bank's business performance and serve community credit needs. Problems arising from failures in any of these areas represent the board's failure to properly exercise its oversight responsibilities and can result in individual liability.

ESTABLISH AN APPROPRIATE CORPORATE CULTURE

The board of directors must create a corporate culture and work environment that supports and encourages responsible, professional, and ethical behavior. The board must commit to establish an ethical culture that acknowledges and maintains an effective internal control environment and risk management system. The board and senior management must establish this culture by upholding corporate integrity and enforcing zero tolerance for compromised ethics. Directors should understand that their and management's actions and behaviors reflect their attitudes about and commitment to integrity, honesty, and ethical conduct. This "tone at the top" shapes corporate culture and permeates the bank's relationships with its shareholders, employees, customers, suppliers, local communities, and other constituents.

The adoption of a written code of ethics and business conduct is a fundamental step in establishing the ethical culture of a bank and designed to prevent unethical and fraudulent behavior within the bank. The board is responsible for overseeing the development, periodic review, and monitoring of the code of ethics and other insider policies that address conduct, conflicts of interest, and other relevant issues. Such a code is intended to focus the board and management on areas of ethical risk, provide guidance so personnel can recognize and deal with ethical issues, and help foster a culture of honesty and accountability.

The code of ethics should establish guidelines and provide practical examples on the following topics:

☐ Conflicts of interest.

☐ Corporate opportunities.

☐ Self-dealing and acceptance of gifts or favors.

☐ Confidentiality of proprietary and customer information.

☐ Fair dealing.

☐ Protection and proper use of bank assets.

☐ Integrity of books and records.

☐ Vacation policies.

☐ Compliance with laws, rules, and regulations (including insider trading laws).

☐ Reporting any illegal or unethical behavior; i.e., a "whistle-blower" policy.

The code of ethics should identify an ethics officer, bank counsel, or some other individual from whom employees can seek advice in ethically ambiguous situations. The code of ethics should require all directors to disclose all conflicts of interest—no matter how small—to the entire board. All directors should be required to sign a statement acknowledging receipt and understanding of the code of ethics.

The board and executive management set the tone for risk taking. A culture that encourages risks without controls can set the stage for unethical behavior and fraud. In order for strong controls to be an integral part of day-to-day operations, the board and management must take steps to provide a clear bank-wide understanding and appreciation of risk management.

HIRE AND RETAIN COMPETENT MANAGEMENT

A profitable and sound bank is the result of talented and capable management. Effective management has the ability to manage day-to-day operations to achieve the bank's performance goals. Such management has the industry expertise to help the board plan for the bank's future in a changing and competitive marketplace as well as generate new and innovative ideas for board consideration. Effective management has the technical expertise to design and administer the systems and controls necessary to carry out the bank's policies, manage risks, and ensure compliance with laws and regulations.

One of the board's most fundamental responsibilities, therefore, is to select and retain competent management. When a bank hires a chief executive officer (CEO), the board or a designated board committee should actively manage the selection process. Selection criteria should include integrity, technical competence, character, and experience in the financial services industry. The board's choice for a CEO should share the board's operating philosophy and vision for the bank to ensure that mutual trust and a close working relationship are maintained.

The board should consider a formal performance appraisal process to supervise management's performance. Such a process helps to ensure that periodic evaluations take place and demonstrates that the board is fulfilling its responsibility to supervise management. Performance appraisals should evaluate criteria relevant to each position, such as

- ☐ The bank's record of complying with laws and regulations.

- ☐ Criticisms contained in audit and examination reports and their resolution.

- ☐ Management's responsiveness to board directives, including compliance with board-approved policies.

- ☐ The timeliness, quality, and accuracy of management's recommendations and reports.

- ☐ Management's presentations to the board.

- ☐ The bank's business success, including business performance indicators used by bank management—such as actual versus projected performance, comparative bank performance, and peer group comparisons.

The board should review the performance of the CEO and other selected senior officers, as appropriate. In addition, the board should consider requiring performance appraisals for all bank employees. Compensation and benefit packages should contain reasonable terms and conditions and not discriminate against any individuals or groups. They must not be excessive or lead to material financial loss or excessive risk taking for the bank. While the board may want to consider the compensation and benefit packages of similarly situated banks, the board should tailor the compensation package to the bank's size and financial condition, and the nature, scope, and complexities of its operation.

The board or a designated committee should monitor personnel turnover rates to evaluate whether the bank is retaining the expertise and human resources needed to fulfill its goals. The board also should verify that the bank has adequate training programs to support needed skill levels and to keep personnel up-to-date on developments in the financial services industry.

The board should develop a management succession policy to address the loss of the CEO and other key executives. This policy should identify critical positions and qualified potential, including interim, replacements. If no individual in the bank is suitable, the succession policy should identify a temporary replacement (often a director) who could serve until the board finds a successor. The board should review these contingency plans annually to determine if they remain workable.

If the board needs to dismiss a member of the bank's management for poor performance, dishonesty, conflicts of interest, or other reasons and it fails to do so, this failure may represent a serious breach of the board's responsibilities. Management employment contracts that explicitly state the board's statutory authority to remove a member of the bank's management can clarify the board's right to act.

INCENTIVE COMPENSATION

Incentive compensation can be a useful tool in the successful management of a bank. However, compensation programs can provide executives and employees with incentives to take imprudent risks that are inconsistent with the long-term health of a bank. Incentive compensation programs at banks should be supported by strong corporate governance, including active and effective oversight by the board of directors. The board is ultimately responsible for ensuring that a bank's incentive compensation programs for all employees, not solely senior executives, are appropriately balanced and do not jeopardize the bank's safety and soundness. The boards of banks that use incentive compensation to a significant degree should actively oversee the development and operation of incentive compensation policies, systems, and related control processes. Smaller banks that are not significant users of incentive compensation should have programs tailored to their size and complexity of operations.

A sound incentive compensation program should be developed using three overarching principles:

☐ Balanced risk-taking incentives.

☐ Compatibility with effective controls and risk management.

☐ Strong corporate governance.

The board should have access to a level of expertise and experience in risk management and compensation practices in the financial services sector that is appropriate for the nature, scope, and complexity of the bank's activities. The board should also ensure that the bank's risk management function is involved in the design and administration of the incentive compensation program. The board should ensure that the design of the incentive compensation program balances risk and financial results in a manner that prevents employees from exposing the bank to imprudent risks.[6]

Given the key role of senior executives in managing the overall risk-taking activities of an organization, the board should directly approve compensation programs involving senior executives and closely monitor payments relative to risk outcomes. The board should also approve and document any material exceptions or adjustments to the incentive compensation programs established for senior executives and should carefully consider and monitor the effects of any approved exceptions or adjustments to the programs.

The structure, composition, and resources of the board of directors should be constructed to permit effective oversight of the bank's incentive compensation programs. Banks should establish a compensation committee that reports to the board to administer the organization's incentive compensation programs. Smaller banks with less complex incentive compensation programs may not find it necessary or appropriate to require specially tailored board expertise or to retain and use outside experts in this area.

---

[6] Under the Dodd-Frank Wall Street Reform and Consumer Protection Act, the OCC will be issuing regulations or guidance prohibiting any type of incentive-based compensation that encourages inappropriate risk taking by providing an executive officer, employee, director, or principal shareholder with excessive compensation, fees, or benefits; or that could lead to material financial loss to the bank.

BE AWARE OF THE BANK'S OPERATING ENVIRONMENT

Directors should understand generally both the bank's business environment and the legal and regulatory framework within which the bank's activities operate. Rapid and ongoing changes in the financial services industry require this understanding to keep the bank healthy and competitive.

Laws and regulations governing banking effectively impose on bank directors a potential for personal liability. Because of the breadth and importance of these laws, directors should be familiar with them and should determine that the bank has appropriate policies and procedures to maintain compliance with them.

These laws and regulations subject the banking industry to comprehensive regulation. This regulatory scheme addresses, among other things:

☐ Markets served.

☐ Permissible products and services.

☐ Permissible investments.

☐ Dividend restrictions.

☐ Transactions with affiliates.

☐ Capital requirements.

☐ Geographic location.

☐ Lending limit to a single borrower.

☐ Transactions with directors and other insiders.

By working with management, directors can stay informed about economic and industry trends or other matters. For example, they can participate in the following:

☐ Management presentations on bank activities and developments in the industry.

- Bank counsel briefings or reports on legislative and regulatory changes, pending litigation, and emerging compliance issues or other legal developments.

- Bank auditor briefings on major accounting or tax developments.

Other sources of expertise can keep the board up-to-date on issues and trends affecting the bank's operating environment. National trade associations, state bankers' groups, management consultants, correspondent banks, and other professionals can help a board identify and understand emerging problems in the industry and recommend solutions. Industry organizations, for example, offer information and training on legislative and regulatory changes, emerging compliance and risk issues, new products or services, technological advances, or problem areas. The OCC and other bank regulatory agencies also provide general guidance on emerging issues.

MAINTAIN APPROPRIATE RELATIONSHIPS WITH THE PARENT HOLDING COMPANY AND BANK SUBSIDIARIES

A bank that is part of a holding company often has a different operating environment from an independent bank. A bank holding company can be a source of strength for its subsidiary banks and may determine policies and perform key bank functions. The holding company's directors may oversee and review the role and responsibilities of a subsidiary bank's board of directors. A director who serves on the board of both a bank and its holding company must comply with the director's fiduciary duties to the bank, including the duty of loyalty. This duty bars conflicts of interest that may arise when actions that are in the best interest of the holding company conflict with those that are in the best interest of the bank.

For its part, the primary duty of the subsidiary bank's board of directors is to protect the bank. The bank's board must carefully review holding company policies that affect the bank to ensure that they adequately serve the bank. The board is responsible for either approving or recording its lack of approval of holding company directives that affect the bank and then monitoring those directives. If the board is concerned that the holding company is engaging in practices that either may harm the bank or are otherwise inappropriate, the board should notify the holding company and discuss modifications. If the holding company's board does not respond to the bank's concerns, the bank's board should dissent on the record and consider action to protect the bank. The bank's board should hire an independent legal counsel or accountant if it decides it is necessary. The board also may raise its concerns with bank supervisors.

A diversified bank holding company that has nonbank subsidiaries raises additional concerns that a bank board must consider. For example, the board of a holding company's subsidiary bank should be aware of the activities and condition of its holding company affiliates. No bank operates in a vacuum, and an affiliate's unsafe and unsound activities could adversely affect the bank's reputation as well as its condition. Certain transactions with affiliates may not be in the best interests of the bank and, in some cases, may be unlawful. These may include unearned or excessive management or servicing fees charged by the holding company or its affiliates, pressure for excessive dividends, or requests that the bank purchase low-quality assets from affiliates (which is specifically prohibited).

The operating environment of a bank with subsidiaries raises other issues. The board at the bank level must oversee the subsidiaries and verify that effective controls are maintained. Representation on the subsidiary's board is one way to be certain that the bank's board participates in policy making. The bank's board should confirm that it has authority to audit operations and review findings of the subsidiary's own internal or external auditors.

MAINTAIN AN APPROPRIATE BOARD STRUCTURE

The board must ensure that it has an organizational structure to keep it informed and to provide it with adequate support. The board should carefully consider the extent and nature of the demands that are placed on it and should identify areas that committees could appropriately address. Board committees allow for a division of labor and enable directors with the requisite expertise to handle matters that require detailed review or in-depth consideration. Committees may make decisions on the board's behalf or submit recommendations for its consideration, depending on their specific charters.

Committees also help directors get involved and give them important insights to help them oversee the activities of the bank. Participation in committee meetings gives directors an opportunity to consider issues thoroughly and better understand the activities of bank management. Overlapping committee memberships can help integrate board activities.

Each committee should have a clear statement of its mission, authority, responsibility, and duration. Committee charters help ensure that important board functions are not neglected because of misunderstandings or incomplete delegations. Standing committees may address ongoing responsibilities. Ad hoc committees may handle special projects, allowing in-depth consideration of one-time issues.

Committees should report regularly to the board. The entire board is ultimately responsible for all board and committee decisions. The board must assure itself that the committee acted responsibly and its recommendations are reasonable.

The best committee structure for a bank depends on the bank's size, scope of operation, and risk profile, the board's composition, and individual directors' expertise. Board committees typically oversee the bank's risk management by ensuring that management has implemented

☐ Sound policies and procedures, either written or verbal.

☐ Accurate and reliable risk measurement systems.

☐ Timely and meaningful risk reporting processes.

☐ Effective risk controls, such as policy limits, authorizations, and product approvals.

Some committees are required by regulation. An audit committee is required for any bank with assets in excess of $500 million and must be composed entirely of outside directors. A trust audit committee is required for a bank with trust powers. Audit, compensation, and corporate governance/nominating committees are required for banks whose securities are registered with the SEC or the OCC and must be composed entirely of independent directors.[7]

EXECUTIVE COMMITTEE

An executive committee generally is authorized to act for the board in its absence. Large institutions and banks with large boards most commonly have executive committees. This committee usually handles matters requiring board review that arise between board meetings. Executive committees can relieve the board of detailed reviews of information and operational activities. Generally, all major bank functions are subject to review and approval by the executive committee. The executive committee coordinates the work of other board committees. An executive committee, however, should not have the authority to exercise all board powers; for example, the board generally reserves the right to execute extraordinary contracts such as mergers and acquisitions.

AUDIT COMMITTEE

An audit committee performs a key role because it oversees the audit function and financial reporting processes and helps strengthen communication between management and the auditors. The audit committee also often oversees risk management and compliance with the laws and regulations affecting the bank. Because the audit committee evaluates bank operations, outside directors should serve on this committee whenever possible. National banks with assets in excess of $500 million at the beginning of the fiscal year must have an audit committee made up entirely of outside directors.

---

[7] The definition of "independence" varies depending on whether the bank is a public company and on which exchange its stock is listed. The board should consult legal counsel if it is unsure of the requirements.

The audit committee of a large bank must include members with banking or related financial expertise. The committee must have access to its own outside counsel, and the audit committee may not include any large customers of the bank. In certain circumstances, these requirements may be met at the holding company level.[8]

The audit committee should supervise the audit function directly to verify that auditors, internal and external, are independent of bank management and are objective in their findings. The committee should work with these auditors to verify that the bank has comprehensive audit coverage. The committee should hire senior audit personnel, set compensation, review audit plans, and evaluate performance. It should seek to retain auditors who are fully qualified to audit the kinds of activities in which the bank engages. The committee may meet with the bank's examiners as necessary, sometimes without management, to review reports and discuss findings. Finally, the committee should monitor management's efforts to correct deficiencies described in an audit or a regulatory examination.

In addition to traditional audit functions, the audit committee may be a vehicle for communicating risk management concerns to the board. The audit committee should ensure that risk management evaluation functions are independent, because the objective is to evaluate management's ability to manage risk within the policies established by the board of directors. As a result, many banks have a requirement that risk management findings be reported directly to the board's audit committee. The audit committee may also be responsible for overseeing internal loan review.

---

[8] For additional information regarding audit committee requirements, including those of public companies, refer to the "Internal and External Audits" booklet of the *Comptroller's Handbook*.

LOAN COMMITTEE

A loan committee ensures that management's handling of credit risk complies with board decisions about acceptable levels of risk. The committee reviews the bank's lending policies and monitors the lending officers' compliance with such policies. It verifies that management follows appropriate procedures to recognize adverse trends, to identify problems in the loan portfolio early, to take corrective actions, and to maintain an adequate allowance for loan and lease losses (ALLL). The committee should determine that risk controls are in place governing compliance with loan-related or other applicable laws and regulations. In many banks, this committee also evaluates credit applications and helps make credit decisions, especially for credits involving large dollar amounts.

ASSET/LIABILITY MANAGEMENT COMMITTEE

An asset/liability management committee's primary responsibility is to oversee the bank's actions relating to interest rate risk and liquidity risks. The committee may be responsible for overseeing controls to manage price and compliance risks.

Among other activities, the committee typically reviews interest rate risk exposures and approves management strategies for investment securities activities, derivatives transactions, deposit programs, and lending initiatives. It evaluates the bank's liquidity position and assesses how anticipated changes may affect that position. Asset/ liability management committees in more complex banks may approve trading strategies and review trading positions in securities, derivatives, or foreign exchange. If the bank's broker-dealer business subjects the bank to the rules of the Municipal Securities Rulemaking Board or rules implementing the Government Securities Act, the committee also typically reviews compliance activities relating to these rules.

RISK MANAGEMENT COMMITTEE

At some banks, the traditional loan and asset/liability committees have been replaced with a broader risk management committee responsible for overseeing all of the bank's risk management activities. This type of committee structure promotes an integrated approach to evaluating and monitoring interrelated risks, especially in banks with complex activity and product mixes.

FIDUCIARY COMMITTEES

A national bank with trust powers generally establishes at least two fiduciary committees: one for policy deliberations, and one to oversee fiduciary audit functions. The policy committee, usually called the fiduciary or trust committee, oversees fiduciary activities to ensure that the board meets its responsibilities and the bank complies with the multitude of statutes and regulations governing these activities. The fiduciary committee provides guidance on such matters as the types of fiduciary services offered, fiduciary investment practices, brokerage placement practices, retention of legal counsel, and appropriate fee structures. The committee approves and oversees policies on hiring a staff competent to perform fiduciary activities. Finally, the committee takes all necessary steps to avoid conflicts of interest between the bank, its directors, officers, and employees and the fiduciary interests of customers and beneficiaries.

A fiduciary audit committee, separate from the fiduciary committee, oversees the annual or continuous audits of the bank's fiduciary activities. The fiduciary audit committee reviews controls for operational, reputation, and compliance risks as they relate to fiduciary activities. All national banks with fiduciary powers must have a fiduciary audit committee, although this committee may be combined with the audit committee.

COMPENSATION COMMITTEE[9]

A compensation committee determines that the bank's compensation and benefits packages are aligned with prudent risk taking and do not provide excessive benefits or lead to material financial loss to the bank. Because of potential conflicts of interest, only outside directors should serve on this committee whenever possible. The committee

---

[9] Specific requirements for compensation committees are to be issued at a later date, as prescribed by the Dodd-Frank Wall Street Reform and Consumer Protection Act.

approves or recommends to the board compensation and benefits packages or plans for management, directors, and employees. These compensation and benefits packages may include salaries, bonuses, incentive compensation, vacations, termination benefits, profit-sharing plans, contributions to employee pension plans, stock option and stock purchase plans, and indemnification agreements. When reviewing these plans, the committee should consider the following issues:

- [ ] Combined value of all cash and noncash benefits provided to the individual.

- [ ] Compensation history of the individual and other individuals with comparable expertise at the bank.

- [ ] The bank's financial condition.

- [ ] Comparable compensation practices at similar institutions, based on such factors as asset size, geographic location, and complexity of business activities.

- [ ] Projected total cost and benefit to the bank for post-employment benefits.

- [ ] Any connection between the individual and any fraudulent act or omission, breach of trust or fiduciary duty, or insider abuse with regard to the bank.

CORPORATE GOVERNANCE/NOMINATING COMMITTEE

A nominating committee generally recommends nominees for election as directors and may recommend successors to key management positions when positions become vacant. The committee may develop a management succession plan that specifies key management positions and qualified potential replacements. A larger bank may have a succession plan that addresses positions ranging from middle management to the CEO, while a smaller bank's plan may address only potential successors to the CEO. The committee also should appoint temporary replacements when key positions become vacant. (In smaller banks, a director is sometimes appointed as a temporary replacement.)

Over time, the nominating committee's function has been expanded to provide leadership in shaping a bank's corporate governance practices by overseeing the composition, structure, compensation, and evaluation of the board and its committees. In this expanded role, the governance/nominating committee's primary responsibility is to safeguard the board's independence. In addition, the committee may oversee and review the bank's processes for providing information to the board, including the information's quality and timeliness.

MONITOR OPERATIONS

Although the board may depend on management's expertise to run the bank's daily operations, the board remains ultimately responsible for monitoring the bank's operations. The board can monitor the bank's operations through management reports, but it must do more than merely accept and review these reports; it must be confident that they are accurate, reliable, and contain sufficient details to allow effective monitoring.

The board and bank management must work together to promote the bank's best interests. Both must understand that management works for the board—the board does not work for management. When management dictates the actions for the board to take, the board neither fulfills its responsibilities nor serves the bank well.

While they support each other, the board and management have their own distinct roles and responsibilities. The board should ascertain that lines of authority are clear and that management understands and carries out board policies and directives.

The board should ensure that management has incorporated a sound system of internal controls into the bank's daily operating procedures. Internal controls are designed to safeguard assets, ensure the accuracy and reliability of data, ensure compliance with policies and laws and regulations, and promote management efficiency. Internal controls include basic precautions, such as ensuring proper separation of duties—those responsible for physical custody of an asset should not also be responsible for accounting for it—and verifying accounting data.

AUDIT PROGRAM

A board may evaluate whether it is meeting its oversight responsibilities through a comprehensive audit and control program. Generally, the audit program consists of an ongoing internal audit function and an external audit.

Federal regulation requires that the audit address certain specific areas. The internal audit should provide an ongoing focus on internal controls and a periodic review of all aspects of bank operations. The internal audit should review compliance with approved policies, applicable laws, and regulations. Although the board should decide how frequently the internal audit function needs to review specific operations, areas suitable for more frequent scrutiny include those that present the greatest inherent risks or that have shown weaknesses in past reviews.

If the board or audit committee determines that an external audit is appropriate, it should select an external auditor experienced in the types of activities in which the bank engages. The value of the auditor's judgment depends to a large extent on the auditor's understanding of the issues being reviewed. For example, if a bank is considering expanding into swaps, futures, and options, the board should be certain that the auditor is qualified to assess resulting risks and management techniques.

FULL-SCOPE AUDIT

Many banks have chosen an independent public accountant to conduct full-scope audits of their annual financial statements. This type of audit can provide the board with an objective, third-party opinion on the adequacy of management systems and accounting controls and the accuracy of financial information. In addition to the auditor's opinion regarding financial statements, the board should expect to receive a management letter and possibly other reports highlighting control or other weaknesses identified during the audit.

Federal regulation requires that an independent public accountant prepare an annual report and financial statement for banks with total assets greater than $500 million. For banks that are owned by a holding company, the audited financial statements requirement may be satisfied at the holding company level provided that the consolidated total assets of the bank (or all the holding company's insured depository institution subsidiaries) comprise 75 percent or more of the consolidated total assets of the holding company as of the beginning of its fiscal year. The same regulation also requires that this audit address certain specific areas, such as insider activities. Regulations require audits of fiduciary activities in all national banks exercising trust powers. Full-scope audits may be required in newly chartered banks, banks subject to securities law regulations, and some problem banks. Full-scope audits are strongly encouraged for all other banks.

Federal regulations require the management of public banking companies and national banks with assets greater than $1 billion to assess the effectiveness of the bank's internal control structure and procedures for financial reporting as of the end of every fiscal year. A report by an independent public accountant attesting to management's assessment is also required, except for smaller public banking companies.[10]

Rather than hire an independent public accountant, where permissible the directors of some banks rely on their internal auditors or auditors from their holding company or a correspondent bank to perform their annual audit. The board should be certain that these auditors have the same independence as a public accountant.

LIMITED-SCOPE AUDIT

Because a full-scope audit can involve considerable expense in time and money, some banks use limited-scope reviews. The board (or audit committee) and auditors should agree in advance on the scope of work. These reviews are not full financial audits and do not allow the auditor to render an opinion on the accuracy and completeness of the bank's financial statements. A typical review reports on the adequacy of internal controls and on the accuracy of certain financial information, but normally does not review the loan portfolio or the adequacy of

---

[10] The requirements of the reports differ slightly depending on whether the bank is required to file under the Sarbanes-Oxley Act, 12 CFR 363 Annual Audits and Reporting Requirements, or both. Discussions should be held with the bank's independent public accountant to clarify the requirements.

the ALLL. As a result, the board and the public receive only limited assurance that the bank's reports accurately represent the bank's condition. Therefore, the board should balance the risks against any savings realized when deciding whether to use a limited-scope audit.

ONGOING CONTROL PROGRAM

An ongoing control program helps raise the board's confidence that adequate control of operations has been established. Outside auditors can assist in this function, but many banks find that internal auditors provide an important resource already based within the bank. In such a program, auditors review and test whether the board's operating procedures have adequate controls that function properly and that comply with board policies and laws and regulations. Such auditors also often help management develop strategies to address problems.

Ongoing control programs may reduce the cost of an annual external audit. The external auditor evaluates the internal audit function as part of its audit. If the external auditor finds the internal audit to be reliable, the external auditor may reduce the scope and, as a result, the cost of its audit. The external auditor's evaluation of the quality, reliability, and independence of the bank's internal audit function also provides the board with an informed opinion about the internal auditors' performance.

During its pre-examination planning, OCC examiners review both the internal and external auditors' reports and a sample of internal audit work papers. Examiners sometimes even review the external auditors' work papers and meet with the external auditors. If the OCC deems this work reliable, the examiners generally accept the auditors' conclusions and reduce the amount of time spent in a given area of the bank.

AUDITOR INDEPENDENCE

Regardless of how the board staffs its monitoring responsibilities—whether by external or internal auditors or a combination—it is critical that the board (not management) control the selection, retention, evaluation, and compensation of those performing the audits or reviews. Auditors must have access to the board or its audit committee so that they can directly report their findings. The audit committee should carefully review the auditors' findings and bring key issues to the board's attention. The board should ask management to report periodically on its progress toward resolving problems raised by the audits, so the board can be sure that management is taking the necessary corrective actions. Failure to address identified problems undermines the audit's value and breaches the board's responsibilities.

COMPLIANCE ACTIVITIES

Many banks establish a separate compliance function headed by a compliance officer or committee. A bank's compliance function may focus on a number of areas, including consumer and antidiscrimination laws, legal lending limit, tax, and securities issues. The compliance officer or committee generally performs periodic compliance reviews, develops necessary systems and controls, assesses the impact of new laws and regulations on bank operations and procedures, and provides guidance on compliance issues as the bank develops new products. For example, a compliance officer may develop appropriate procedures for complying with insider lending regulations, the consumer protection laws, and regulations governing bank securities dealer activities.

Compliance officers should provide appropriate training for bank employees on compliance issues. Larger, more complex banks generally have more elaborate compliance functions than smaller, less complex banks. The board should actively support the compliance function.

The BSA requires banks to establish a compliance program to fulfill its recordkeeping and reporting requirements and to confirm the identity of bank customers. Broadly, the objective of the program is to prevent a bank from becoming a conduit for money laundering and terrorist financing activity. The BSA compliance program must be written, approved by the board, and reflected in the minutes of the bank. The program shall include internal operating controls to monitor and report suspicious activity, independent testing of bank activities and transactions for compliance, training for employees, and an individual(s) designated to coordinate and monitor day-to-day compliance activities.

INFORMATION TECHNOLOGY ACTIVITIES

Banks rely heavily on information technology (IT) to process bank transactions and to supply reports to management and the board about managing business risk. The board must ensure that the information provided by management in IT reports is accurate, timely, and sufficiently detailed to oversee the bank's safe and sound operation. Board and management responsibilities include vendor management and safeguarding customers' nonpublic information.

The board should actively demonstrate that it understands the bank's IT infrastructure, inherent risks, and existing controls. In some banks, there is a chief technology officer and an information security officer. The information security officer reports directly to the board. Both the chief technology officer and the information security officer should provide periodic updates on the bank's IT infrastructure and operations to the board.

The board should review and approve adequate disaster recovery and business continuity plans every year. Sound business continuity plans allow banks to respond to such adverse events as natural disasters, technology failures, human error, and terrorism. Banks must be able to restore information systems, operations, and customer services quickly and reliably after any adverse event. It is important that business operations be resilient and that customer service disruptions be minimized.

The board should also review and approve an adequate information security program annually, or as frequently as it is necessary to revise the program based on known vulnerabilities and threats. A robust risk assessment drives the information security program. The risk assessment provides guidance for the selection and implementation of security controls and the timing and nature of testing those controls. Testing can validate the basis for accepting risks. The board should understand and acknowledge any gaps between identified risks and existing controls.

CONFIDENTIAL REPORTING SYSTEM

A bank's financial condition and good reputation depend not only on the honesty and integrity of management and the workforce but also on the reporting of lapses in honesty and integrity by those who witness such behavior. The existence of a confidential reporting system indicates that the board gives prompt attention to ethics lapses and other inappropriate or illegal activity. Having such a system emphasizes the responsibility that all employees have for leadership and ethical behavior—including reporting suspected wrongdoing.

The Sarbanes-Oxley Act requires public banking companies to implement a confidential system for reporting information regarding questionable accounting or auditing matters, known as the "whistle-blower" provision. Such a system might also be used to report suspected violations of the code of ethics and business conduct and to report other workplace issues, including any operational problems, inappropriate conduct, policy violations, or other risks to the bank.

Boards should consider the benefits of implementing several reporting platforms, such as discussions with supervisors, confidential conversations with human resources professionals, secure company Web sites and e-mail, and anonymous tip lines.

Any claim that has the potential to materially affect the financial statements should be referred to the audit committee. Complaints that have merit but are not relevant to the financial statements (for example, personnel grievances) can be referred to other parties in the bank for review and handling.

OVERSEE BUSINESS PERFORMANCE

Sound business performance is one of the board's primary objectives and responsibilities and a key indicator of management's success. A bank is in business to offer financial services to its community and to earn a return on its shareholders' investments. Consistently poor earnings performance affects this return and can hinder the bank's ability to generate capital to support growth.

Sound financial performance means more than simply how much the bank earned last quarter. Equally important is the quality of earnings over the long term. Quality earnings result from sound fundamentals: good quality assets, stable funding sources, well-controlled expenses, sound asset/liability management practices, and knowledge of markets served. When evaluating the quality of earnings, directors should understand the soundness of the bank's operations and the interrelationships among operating statistics. Directors should ensure, for instance, that the bank does not artificially inflate earnings by delaying chargeoffs or inadequately providing for loan and lease losses. Auditors' reports and reports from the bank's independent loan review program are helpful when evaluating the reliability of management's figures.

A board should receive adequate financial data and analyses that can answer such questions as:

☐ Is management meeting the goals established in the planning process? If not, why not?

☐ Was the plan unrealistic because of the circumstances?

☐ Is the level of earnings consistent or erratic?

☐ Do earnings result from the implementation of planned bank strategies or from transactions designed to increase short-term earnings but that also raise longer-term risk?

☐ Is the bank being adequately compensated for the risks it is taking in its product lines and activities?

☐ Does the bank have sufficient capital to support its risk profile and business strategies?

☐ Are the reports accurate or do they reflect an incomplete evaluation of asset quality or expenses?

The board is in a better position to answer these questions if it receives reports highlighting key performance measures, trends, and anomalies rather than being deluged with large amounts of raw data. The board should identify the reports it wants to receive from management and their frequency. Key performance reports should enable the board to evaluate the amount of risk being taken, compliance with the board's risk tolerances, and the adequacy of the bank's risk management processes. The bank's management information systems should reflect these requirements and provide up-to-date reports in a timely manner.

Useful reports are likely to include the following information: budgeted compared with actual performance; portfolio activity, including classified asset trends, significant loans, past dues, and renewals; liquidity trends; off-balance-sheet exposures, including derivatives activities; concentrations in assets and funding sources; and interest rate sensitivity reports.

It is often helpful for the board to compare results with those of the bank's peer group. The quarterly Uniform Bank Performance Report (UBPR), which is derived from call report data and is provided to each national bank, compares the bank's performance with an identified peer group. Although deviations from peer group norms do not necessarily indicate problems, management should explain large differences. Understanding the reasons for the differences helps the board determine whether there is a problem.

The board should realize, however, that peer group averages are not a benchmark, merely an analytical tool. There are no model ratios or numbers that guarantee success. The peer group data simply tell how banks of similar size and complexity are performing in certain areas of their operations. Peer group data do not necessarily indicate good or appropriate performance and may not reflect the same goals as the bank.

KEY MEASURES OF BUSINESS PERFORMANCE

Certain key financial ratios, although not all-inclusive, provide good insight into bank and management performance. Some of these ratios, which are available in the UBPR, include the following.

Return on average assets (ROAA). Net income divided by average assets. This is the primary profitability indicator and measures the bank's efficiency in using its assets to generate profits. A ratio that is significantly above banks in similar markets offering similar products can be one indicator that the bank is taking above average risk.

Return on equity (ROE). Net income divided by equity capital. Investors use this ratio to measure the return on the shareholder's investment. This ratio is also important when calculating the bank's value to potential investors. From the shareholder's perspective, the higher the ROE the better. From the board's perspective, however, it should not seek an attractive ROE that is based on inadequate capital or unwarranted risk.

Net interest margin (NIM). Interest income less interest expense divided by average earning assets. This ratio reflects the traditional business of banking, that is, the results of the bank's efforts to buy funds and reinvest them profitably.

Net noninterest expense to average assets. Total noninterest income less total noninterest expense divided by average assets. This ratio indicates the impact of all noninterest expenses (such as personnel, occupancy, or other costs) on the bank's earnings and can provide a measure of the bank's efficiency in generating earnings.

Leverage ratio. Tier 1 capital (as defined in the OCC's capital regulations) divided by average assets. This ratio indicates how much Tier 1 capital is available to support bank assets and future growth. Capital provides a cushion against unexpected losses and promotes public confidence in the bank's condition. Confidence in the bank's condition is a critical factor in its ability to attract deposits and support further business. Thus, although regulatory guidelines establish minimum capital requirements that banks must meet, well-managed banks typically operate with more capital than these minimum requirements.

A declining leverage ratio is frequently an indication of large loan losses, rapid asset growth, or large dividend payouts. A declining leverage ratio also may reflect a loss of profitability because of such factors as the absence of cost controls, inadequate pricing, or a flawed business plan. The board should set as a floor the minimum leverage ratio for the bank (a ratio at least equal to regulatory requirements). The board should be alert to any declines in the ratio and should determine the cause and take necessary action to ensure that adequate capital is maintained.

Nonperforming loans to total loans. Loans that are past due at least 90 days, are in nonaccrual status, or have been renegotiated divided by the total loan portfolio. A high level of nonperforming loans may suggest poor underwriting practices or inadequate monitoring of changes in borrowers' financial conditions. The bank should determine the cause of an increase in nonperforming loans and institute appropriate corrective actions.

Net losses to average total loans. Loan losses after recoveries divided by average total loans. This ratio is another indicator of asset quality. An increasing ratio may indicate that the ALLL is being depleted by increasing losses; thus, additional provisions to the ALLL may be necessary. Increasing losses also may reflect severe deterioration in the loan portfolio, management's inability to identify loan problems in their early stages, or management's inability to develop strong workout and collection programs for problem loans. The bank should determine the cause of the increased losses and take appropriate corrective actions.

BUSINESS PERFORMANCE: KEY AREAS TO MONITOR

Monitoring these financial ratios keeps the board aware of the bank's business performance. In addition, the board should keep the following key areas in mind when overseeing a bank's business performance.

ASSET QUALITY

Because a bank's condition can depend in large part on its ability to control credit risk, the board or its loan committee should closely monitor internal loan review findings and issues identified in an external audit report or the OCC's Report of Examination. Any weaknesses should be addressed in a timely fashion before they become more serious. Issues that may raise concerns include a rapid increase in loan volume, concentrations of credit, the purchase of large numbers of participations from outside the bank's normal trade area, or failure to timely recognize asset impairments and establish adequate reserves. If this occurs, the board should ascertain that credit quality does not suffer and that the bank's systems are adequate to monitor or service such loans. Also, if the board accepts higher risk as part of the bank's risk strategy, the board should be certain that the bank is adequately compensated and this risk is properly managed.

LIQUIDITY AND INTEREST RATE RISK POSITIONS

The board must make certain that the bank's liquidity and interest rate risk positions are reasonable and do not compromise the bank's ability to maintain earnings and protect capital. While accepting some degree of interest rate risk and maturity mismatch is inherent to the business of banking, the board and management must understand and control the risks that the bank takes. Such risks must be commensurate with management's expertise and the bank's balance sheet flexibility, especially since rapidly changing market conditions can have a substantial impact on the bank's position.

Useful indicators of risk positions include the extent of the bank's dependence on volatile liabilities, concentrations in funding, the level of mismatch between the bank's asset and liability cash flows, and the vulnerability of earnings and capital to movements in interest rates. The board should be aware that such strategies as funding long-term fixed-rate assets with short-term liabilities may enhance earnings in the short run but may threaten earnings and capital if market conditions change or if earnings do not materialize as expected.

NEW PRODUCTS AND SERVICES

The board should be certain that it fully understands the risks presented by any proposed new product or service. If, for example, the pricing does not support a reasonable return in comparison with the risks, the board should question whether the product or service is worth offering. Furthermore, the new product or service should be consistent with the bank's strategic or business plan. The board should verify that management understands the risks of the new product or service, including any compliance or reputation risks, and ensure that adequate policies, procedures, and systems are in place to facilitate the product or service's introduction and ongoing risk management.

NONINTEREST EARNINGS

In many banks, a major component of noninterest earnings is income from fee-based products such as mutual funds, mortgage banking, and fiduciary services. These products can contribute substantially to the bank's income, but they also introduce new concerns and expose the bank to various risks, including operational, compliance, strategic, and reputation risks. The bank must be equipped to service and stand behind its products and to price them realistically and competitively. The bank should perform an effective cost analysis before introducing the product and ensure that adequate management information systems are in place to support the offering. Management also must ensure that it has skilled personnel to administer and support these activities.

Noninterest earnings may reflect the sales of assets or other nonrecurring items. In these cases, the board should ask management to identify noninterest earnings that are inflated by unusual nonrecurring items. Directors should be concerned when nonrecurring transactions supplement earnings to maintain budgeted earnings levels.

OFF-BALANCE-SHEET ITEMS

When evaluating the bank's risk profile and capital position, the board must consider the nature and extent of all off-balance-sheet items, especially items that may ultimately require funding. A loan commitment is an example of an off-balance-sheet item that may require funding. When a bank is experiencing liquidity problems, borrowers typically draw down their commitments to be certain that the funding is available. The board also should understand exposures to any off-balance-sheet derivative contracts, such as swaps, futures, and options, whether used to hedge existing or anticipated positions or used as an alternative investment product to generate earnings.

Management should provide regular reports to the board on all off-balance-sheet activity. These reports should explain the types and amount of risk involved and indicate what internal controls, audit, and monitoring functions are in place to manage risks.

DIVIDENDS

The bank's ability to pay dividends is an indication of its overall health and profitability. Dividends are a source of investment income to shareholders. Banks must, however, strike a proper balance between income for shareholders and the retention of earnings to maintain adequate capital levels. Moreover, federal law prohibits banks from paying dividends that would impair the bank's capital, and banks may need supervisory approval if they wish to pay dividends in excess of certain amounts.

SERVE COMMUNITY CREDIT NEEDS

Every national bank is required to fulfill its responsibilities under the CRA. A board's plans and policies should not only address profits and safety and soundness but also reflect efforts to help meet the legitimate credit needs of all communities the bank serves. Directors frequently represent a cross-section of these communities and thus are in an excellent position to assess community needs and to formulate appropriate, responsive policies.

A bank charter imposes significant responsibilities to serve the community. Under the CRA, bank regulators must review and consider public comments on a bank's record in meeting community credit needs before acting on applications for branches, mergers, and certain other structural changes. The growth of interstate branching and other factors that may affect credit flows to and from local communities have heightened concerns about local community credit needs.

A board is responsible for ensuring that CRA efforts are an important element in a bank's plans and policies and that those efforts focus on performance rather than outreach, marketing, or other aims. The board should encourage management to be innovative and committed to serving the needs of the community in which the bank operates. For many banks, active CRA efforts reflect good corporate citizenship as well as the development of profitable business. A good CRA performance rating can facilitate a bank's expansion plans.

A board should evaluate whether any areas of the bank's community have credit needs that are unmet and whether any changes to the bank's current plans or policies are appropriate. The board should consider whether otherwise sound policies and procedures could have the unintended effect of discouraging good quality business in older and low- or moderate-income neighborhoods. For example, a policy that places a maximum age limit on structures held as collateral may result in blanket credit denials in the community's older neighborhoods. Such a policy could exclude responsible citizens attempting to rehabilitate housing from even being considered for credit.

The board should work with management to maintain a constructive dialogue with community members. Without good communication, a bank may find itself at odds with its community, even if the board satisfies the CRA's goals. Poor communication also may result in the filing of adverse comments to bank regulators. Often referred to as CRA protests, these adverse comments may cause costly delays for a bank seeking a regulatory decision on a corporate application.

III

THE BOARD'S ROLE IN PLANNING
AND POLICY

PLANNING

POLICIES

MAJOR POLICY AREAS

PLANNING

The board is responsible for establishing the bank's goals and for ensuring that the bank has the personnel as well as the financial, technological, and organizational capabilities to achieve those goals. Ongoing changes in the banking industry make it essential for the bank to have a clear strategic plan as well as business plans.

The planning process typically begins with the development of a long-term strategic plan. The plan usually contains a statement of the board's general philosophy and includes a mission statement or the board's vision of the bank's future. A strategic plan provides a framework for making business judgments and for considering proposals that deviate from the board's stated philosophy. The board should reassess the strategic plan periodically to consider new opportunities or to respond to unanticipated external developments. Larger, more complex banks generally would have more detailed plans than smaller, less complex banks. A small bank operating in a stable environment may only need to set goals and define the basic business of the bank.

Short-term business plans translate long-term goals into specific, measurable targets. Management is often in the best position to formulate these plans. The board should approve these plans after concluding that they are realistic and compatible with the bank's tolerance for risk. The board should consider, for instance, whether the bank's capital and other resources are adequate to achieve the goals and whether management has realistically assessed staff expertise and systems adequacy.

The board should review and approve any proposed departures from the bank's strategic and business plans before they take place. For example, the board should have a planning, review, and approval process for major new activities or products that bank management proposes. Many new undertakings require substantial systems support, new expertise, lead time, and significant financial investment. The board should ensure that bank management has identified potential risks and rewards and established adequate risk management systems to monitor, measure, and control risk and performance. Management or staff assessing the impact of these business plans on overall bank operations should address associated risks.

The planning process should include strategies to meet unanticipated operational contingencies to control strategic risk. Disruptions to operations can include loss of bank premises or automated systems because of fire, flood, or another disaster. The bank's business continuity plan should forecast how departure from a business plan or a major operational loss could affect customer services or bank resources, including expert staff dedicated to the plans. Finally, business continuity plans should address insurance coverage and backup procedures and facilities.

POLICIES

Policies set standards and courses of action to achieve specific goals and objectives established by the board. Policies should be consistent with the bank's underlying mission, values, and principles. They also clarify the bank's tolerance for risk. Statutes, regulations, and certain OCC issuances require written policies governing some activities. In other areas, the decision to put a policy in writing is up to the board, but generally policies should be written for ease of reference and to ensure consistent application. Written or not, all policies need to provide clear guidance and should be effectively communicated throughout the bank. Policies should be flexible enough to permit innovation and let management respond to changing business conditions. Training programs should inform employees of policies and how they should be applied.

Associated procedures detail how the policies are to be implemented. The procedures should include steps for obtaining appropriate approval for policy exceptions.

If policies and procedures are developed by bank management or some other party, the board should ensure that the policies and procedures specifically address the bank's unique goals, systems, personnel, risk tolerance, and resources before giving its approval.

The board or its designated committee should periodically review policies and oversee revisions as necessary to ensure that they remain consistent with the bank's goals and risk tolerance. If the board and management receive many legitimate requests for exceptions, they may need to reconsider the policy. Finally, the board should ensure that bank policies and procedures are modified when necessary to respond to significant changes in the bank's resources, activities, or business conditions.

While all banks should have policies that address their significant activities and risks, the coverage and level of detail of those policies will vary among banks. The OCC generally expects that a smaller, noncomplex bank whose management is heavily involved in day-to-day operations will have basic policies addressing the significant areas of operations and setting forth a limited set of requirements and procedures. In a larger, more complex bank, where senior management must rely on a widely dispersed staff to implement strategies in an extended range of potentially complex businesses, the OCC generally expects to see far more detailed policies and procedures.

Policies and procedures should be in place before any new activity begins. Management should articulate the risks and rewards of new products and services, and the board should not approve any new activity before it fully understands the risks and the potential profitability of the activity. The board should specify appropriate tools to measure and monitor the risks and should have a way to report risks to all responsible parties before the bank engages in a new activity.

MAJOR POLICY AREAS

This section highlights the policy treatment of some important functional areas and identifies issues within these areas that may require special attention.

LOAN PORTFOLIO MANAGEMENT

The board should oversee loan portfolio management to control risks and maintain profitable lending operations. Traditionally, lending has been at the core of a bank's activities, providing the greatest single source of earnings and accounting for the largest volume of assets; however, lending has also posed the greatest single risk to a bank's safety and soundness. Whether because of lax credit standards, inadequate loan review practices, or weaknesses in the economy, loan portfolio problems have been a major cause of bank failures.

LOAN POLICY

A bank's loan policy should address loan portfolio composition and should have standards for individual credit decisions. Risk tolerances and limits should be specified. Elements of a sound loan policy that set parameters for the loan portfolio include:

☐ Portion of the bank's funding sources that may be used for lending.

☐ Types of loans to be made.

☐ Percentage of the overall loan portfolio that should constitute each type of loan.

☐ Geographic trade area in which loans will be made.

☐ Guidance on lending activities outside the defined trade area.

☐ Limits on purchased loans.

☐ Guidelines on insider loans. (These guidelines must be in writing, even if the remainder of the policy is not written.)

- ☐ Individual credit requirements.

- ☐ Loan underwriting criteria.

- ☐ Loan application requirements.

- ☐ Limits on concentrations of credit.

- ☐ Approval authority.

- ☐ Administrative practices.

- ☐ Compliance with lending-related laws and regulations, such as the legal lending limit, real estate lending and appraisal standards, insider lending regulations, CRA, and fair lending laws and regulations.

LOAN REVIEW PROGRAM

In addition to the general loan policy, the board should direct management to establish an internal loan review program that is independent of the lending function. This program, which is essential to managing credit risk, should monitor asset quality, adherence to established loan policy and credit standards, and compliance with laws and regulations.

The loan review function should report directly to the board or its audit committee. Individuals who perform the loan review should not review loans in which they have an interest or loans in which they participated in granting. Loan reviewers should have experience analyzing loans, identifying credit weaknesses, and assessing the degree of risk involved. In larger banks, the loan review function often is organized into a separate department. In smaller banks, loan review can consist of loan officers reviewing one another's loans. Some loan review programs also use internal auditors, other compliance personnel, or outside consultants to assess whether the bank is complying with the board's lending policies and properly identifying problem loans.

The loan review program monitors portfolio trends and analyzes potential risks in the portfolio. The program should quantify the repayment risk in the portfolio by estimating how much cash commercial borrowers could generate from operations or the value of collateral sources under current and adverse market conditions. The bank should have a loan classification system that identifies the likelihood of repayment. The board may want to follow the loan classification system used by the OCC because the judgments the bank and the examiners reach should not be materially different if classification criteria are essentially the same.

The board and management use the information drawn from loan portfolio reviews to assess whether the overall loan policy is effective, to maintain an adequate ALLL, and to serve as an early warning system for identifying underlying problems. For example, improper documentation or continuing violations of lending limits might mean that loan officers need more training or that compliance efforts should be increased. Recurring credit quality problems can pinpoint weaknesses in the performance of individual loan officers or can warn of emerging problems in the local economy or industry sectors. Early warning allows the bank to act before those problems have a major impact.

ALLOWANCE FOR LOAN AND LEASE LOSSES

The board must ensure that the bank has a program for developing, maintaining, and documenting a comprehensive, systematic, and consistently applied process for determining the amounts of the ALLL and the provision for loan and lease losses. To fulfill this responsibility, the board should ensure controls are in place to consistently determine the ALLL in accordance with generally accepted accounting principles (GAAP), the bank's stated policies and procedures, management's best judgment, and relevant supervisory guidance.

As of the end of each quarter, or more frequently if warranted, each bank must analyze the collectibility of its loans and leases held for investment[11] and make entries to maintain the ALLL at an appropriate

---

[11] These are loans and leases that the bank has the intent and ability to hold for the foreseeable future or until maturity or payoff. The ALLL does not apply to loans carried at fair value, loans held for sale, off-balance-sheet credit exposures (e.g., loan commitments, standby letters of credit, and guarantees), or general or unspecified business risks.

level. An appropriate ALLL covers estimated credit losses[12] on individually evaluated loans that are determined to be impaired and estimated credit losses inherent in the remainder of the loan and lease portfolio. The evaluation should be based on management's current judgments about the credit quality of the loan portfolio and should use information from the internal loan review. Management's evaluation is subject to review by examiners.

Because the ALLL provision affects the accuracy of the earnings statement, an understated ALLL expense will overstate the bank's earnings and can result in a violation of law. The board is responsible for overseeing management's significant judgments and estimates pertaining to the determination of an appropriate ALLL. This oversight should include but is not limited to

☐ Reviewing and approving the bank's ALLL policies and procedures at least annually.

☐ Reviewing management's assessment and justification that the loan review program is sound and appropriate for the bank's size and complexity.

☐ Reviewing management's assessment and justification for the amounts estimated and reported each period for the ALLL and the provision for loan and lease losses.

☐ Requiring management to periodically validate and, when appropriate, revise the ALLL methodology.

LOAN PORTFOLIO MANAGEMENT—AREAS OF CONCERN

When considering the bank's lending activities, the board should scrutinize the following practices or conditions.

Failure to have systems that properly monitor compliance with legal lending limits. Violating lending limits can lead to excessive concentrations of risk, may present an opportunity for bank insiders

---

[12] This is the estimate of the current amount of loans that the bank will be unable to collect, given facts and circumstances as of the evaluation date (i.e., net chargeoffs that are likely to be realized).

or affiliates to abuse the bank's resources, and may result in financial liability for directors. Accordingly, the board must direct management to adopt a system to generate accurate and timely reports on the bank's legal lending limits. The reports should identify the limits applicable to all borrowers, including bank insiders and bank affiliates, and should reflect that loan limits were properly considered in loan decisions. Bank management should pay particular attention to circumstances in which loans should be aggregated or attributed to another borrower. Management also should be aware of the circumstances under which the board may be required by law to approve loans to insiders in advance. If a highly complex lending limit transaction is presented or the board or management is uncertain whether a loan approval will exceed the bank's lending limit, the bank should consider obtaining guidance from counsel.

Relaxed standards or terms on loans to insiders and affiliates. Several laws and regulations prohibit banks from providing preferential treatment to insiders and affiliates. Such treatment may subject the bank to unwarranted concentrations of risk or levels of credit risk. The bank also may face legal and financial liability as a result of these activities.

Failure to institute adequate loan administration systems. A bank with an inadequate system to administer its loans can experience unnecessary losses. Management's ongoing assessment of risk in the loan portfolio may be compromised, for example, if current, detailed financial information on borrowers is not maintained. Failure to either perfect collateral positions or to carry out adequate follow-up and collection procedures also can trigger unwarranted risks and lead to otherwise avoidable losses. In addition, if management does not supervise loan performance adequately, management may be unable to evaluate the performance of individual loan officers who could be perpetuating portfolio weaknesses.

Overreliance on collateral or character to support credit decisions. A bank that unduly relies on factors other than cash flow or other repayment capacity to support credit decisions may increase its illiquid loans and its level of credit risk and may expose the bank to loss. Loans not supported by adequate cash flow are often made for speculative purposes and pose greater risks than basic business and personal loans. The board should monitor carefully the bank's exposure to such loans and institute acceptable limits. Proper attention to repayment capacity is critical, even for such lending products as community development loans, unless the loans have government or other support, in which case flexible criteria may be appropriate.

Uncontrolled asset growth or increased market share. One way for a bank to achieve rapid asset growth or increase its market share is to compromise its credit standards. The board should be alert to any activity that could indicate that loan officers are relaxing credit standards. Such practices may result in increases in illiquid assets and unwarranted losses to the bank.

Purchase of participations in out-of-area loans without independent review and evaluation. Some banks purchase out-of-area participations in loans made by other institutions to increase loan volume or to diversify risk. To avoid undue losses, the bank or a party independent of the seller must review and evaluate the quality and concentration risk of such out-of-area participations before purchase.

Generation of large volumes of loans for resale to others. If a bank plans to generate a large volume of loans to sell to others to increase income, the board should ensure that the bank's systems and controls are capable of handling the volume. Also, the board should verify that credit standards have not been lowered, because selling poor quality assets may cause the bank to lose access to the market. Purchasers could subject the bank to legal action or recourse for misrepresenting or improperly administering the loans.

ASSET/LIABILITY MANAGEMENT

The asset/liability management policy provides the framework for bank management to carry out the board's objectives for the composition of on- and off-balance-sheet positions. Policy parameters should be designed to control the actions of management and provide timely feedback to the board. Once the board has specified acceptable risk tolerances, management can begin to translate decisions into meaningful limits.

The policy should address the board's tolerances for interest rate and liquidity risks and should establish procedures for measuring, monitoring, and controlling these risks. Risk tolerances should be based on a realistic assessment of the board's rate-of-return objectives. For example, a board that establishes extremely low tolerances for risk taking should recognize that this decision is likely to reduce the bank's ability to generate higher returns. Such a strategy, however, can reduce return volatility, which may be of primary concern to the board.

When framing the bank's risk tolerances, directors should determine the maximum amount of bank earnings and capital they are willing to allow bank management to place at risk. For interest rate risk tolerances, the board should consider how movements in interest rates may adversely affect the bank's earnings and capital. The bank's projected earnings and capital often are used as a benchmark for evaluating this exposure. When determining liquidity risk tolerances, the board should consider how the bank's inability to meet its obligations when they come due may affect the bank's earnings, capital, and operations.

The asset/liability management policy should specify what products can be used to manage interest rate risk and liquidity positions. For liquidity, the policy might address what types of borrowings (such as federal funds, term federal funds, and term loans) are acceptable and what counterparties are approved (for example, upstream bank federal funds). The policy should specify who can commit the bank to various transactions and when more senior levels of management or the board need to be notified. The board should approve the purchase of tools that can accurately and reliably measure exposures to interest rate risk and liquidity risk. The policy should include a liquidity contingency plan that specifies how the bank will handle a situation of unusual liquidity pressure.

When considering asset/liability management activities, the board should scrutinize the following practices or conditions.

Excessive growth objectives. A bank with excessive growth objectives may engage in activities that unduly increase its exposure to various risks. For example, bank staff may be inclined to purchase lower quality assets for the bank or set up an unprofitable pricing structure to increase business. Such unwise decisions could lead to significant problems in the bank's asset quality, earnings, or liquidity. Excessive growth also may lead to undue leverage and capital inadequate to support the bank's activities.

Heavy dependence on volatile liabilities. Excessive holdings of volatile liabilities, such as large certificates of deposit, out-of-area funding sources, brokered deposits, and other interest-rate sensitive and credit-risk sensitive funding sources may pose problems to the bank. Liquidity concerns triggered by the sudden withdrawal of such deposits can require the costly liquidation of assets. In addition, the bank typically must pay a higher interest rate to attract out-of-area funds, thereby lowering net interest margins on loans and investments made with those funds. Lower margins can create pressures on management to seek higher yielding, and potentially riskier, loans and investments to maintain earnings.

Exposure to a significant number of products with embedded options. Holding significant amounts of assets, liabilities, or off-balance-sheet products with embedded options can expose the bank to unwarranted interest rate and liquidity risks. Embedded options can be found in mortgage-backed securities, nonmaturity deposits, structured notes, structured or callable borrowings or advances, and even traditional retail bank products. The bank's risk measurement tools should adequately capture this exposure so that management can assess how these options may be exercised under various interest rate scenarios.

For example, embedded options incorporated into retail bank products can significantly alter the cash-flow characteristics of the products under different interest rate scenarios. A residential mortgage with a penalty-free prepayment option, for example, gives the bank customer the right to exercise the option at any time, thereby creating uncertainty about the cash flow on the mortgage. Because customers generally exercise this option when they can refinance their mortgages at a lower rate, the bank is left to reinvest in lower yielding assets. Conversely, when market interest rates rise, fewer customers prepay their mortgages, leaving the bank with longer maturity assets and less cash to reinvest at current market rates.

Gaps between asset and liability maturities or between rate-sensitive assets and liabilities at various maturity time frames. Excessive gaps resulting from differences in the repricing dates of assets and liabilities leave the bank vulnerable to impaired earnings and liquidity concerns if interest rates do not move according to projections. Management should monitor closely its use of volatile or short-term variable-rate funding sources to buy illiquid or long-term fixed-rate assets. The board should understand and agree with the interest-rate assumptions underlying management's gap planning.

Asset/liability expansion, both on- or off-balance sheet, without an accompanying increase in capital support. A bank engaging in excessive leveraging activities may be violating capital requirements. Inadequate capital also may make the bank unable to fund or absorb potential exposures. The board should scrutinize the bank's capital position on an ongoing basis to avoid such events.

Failure to diversify assets or funding sources. Concentrations of assets or funding sources can expose a bank to risks including credit, interest rate, liquidity, and reputation. Credit and interest rate exposures can occur in a bank that places undue reliance on particular companies or economic sectors because a downturn in the company or industry may result in losses. Liquidity risk exists for funding sources that depend on one or a few correspondents, large depositors, or depositors tied to certain economic sectors. The board should make sure the bank's policies and practices provide guidelines for diversifying assets and funding sources and for specifying limits on such sources. The board also should periodically monitor the bank's asset and funding concentrations.

Inadequate controls over securitized asset programs. When a bank uses securitized assets to fund banking activities, it improves the marketability of its assets and enhances liquidity. To control risks associated with such programs, however, management should monitor how sales of its high-quality assets affect the strength of the remaining portfolio. Further, the bank should have risk management procedures adequate for its securitization activities, including ensuring compliance with all applicable accounting and regulatory capital guidelines. For example, management should consider limits on loan and investor concentrations when the bank retains some liability on the asset sold. Management should also consider the bank's ability to access this market and have contingency plans in place to minimize the risk of disruptions to the bank's ability to access this market.

Lack of expertise or control over off-balance-sheet derivative activities or other complex investment or risk management transactions. The growth of various off-balance-sheet derivative contracts—such as swaps, futures, and options, as well as structured note products—provides banks with an increasing array of financial instruments that can be used to manage their risk exposures. Such products can be used to change the timing, direction, or level of a bank's risk. Some products may have complex cash flow and risk characteristics and may introduce additional leverage to the bank's risk profile. The board should be aware of potential risks and ensure that adequate risk monitoring and control procedures are in place before the bank uses the products. The board and management should understand the role such leverage transactions play within the bank's overall business strategies.

INVESTMENT ACTIVITIES

Investments traditionally have been a bank's second largest source of income. Investments should generate quality earnings, allow a bank to diversify its asset base, and provide liquidity. Investment activities are subject to complex legal requirements. These requirements affect the types and amounts of investments banks may make. The board must ensure the bank's investment activities comply with these legal requirements.

While the board may seek advice from technically competent managers or external sources, such as correspondent banks, brokerage houses, or consulting services, the board may not delegate its responsibility for overseeing the investment portfolio. The investment policy should state that the bank must comply with legal restrictions on the types of securities the bank may hold. The policy also should specify the type and composition (including the maturity and repricing characteristics) of those instruments. Factors such as the bank's earnings, ability to accept risk, liquidity needs, pledging requirements, funding sources, and income objectives help define the board's policy objectives. The board should review the portfolio as necessary to confirm that the risk level remains acceptable and consistent with previously approved portfolio objectives. The review should include information on the current market value of the portfolio and consideration of whether the investment policy needs to be revised.

The board should direct management to establish systems with objectives and limits for each portfolio, taking into account applicable laws, regulations, and current accounting standards for each part of the portfolio. The bank's risk management systems should enable management to evaluate how changes in market factors, such as interest rates, may affect the value of the bank's investment portfolios, especially securities with embedded options. The risk management systems should be capable of monitoring and controlling other risks associated with investment activities, such as credit, liquidity, operational, compliance, strategic, and reputation.

INVESTMENT ACTIVITIES—AREAS OF CONCERN

When considering investment activities, the board should scrutinize the following practices or conditions.

Failure to select securities dealers carefully. Management should be aware of the credit standing, record, and reputation of securities dealers with whom the bank does business. The board should reaffirm a list of approved securities dealers annually to ensure that the bank does not deal with financially unstable, irresponsible, or dishonest securities dealers.

Efforts to obtain higher yields without regard for other portfolio objectives. The bank should not extend the investment portfolio's maturity to obtain higher yields without carefully considering liquidity and funding issues. Extending maturities without evaluating these issues increases liquidity and interest rate risks because unanticipated liquidity demands may lead to the sale of securities at depressed market prices. In addition, interest rate movements or changes in quality can cause the value of securities to decline.

Purchase of low-quality investments to obtain higher yields. Low-quality investments are highly volatile because they can experience wide price fluctuations as interest rates or other investor expectations change. Purchasing these investments also increases credit risk. Lower quality investments also impair the bank's liquidity and reduce flexibility in managing the investment portfolio.

Purchase of structured securities without appropriate due diligence. Complex, structured investments, often purchased to support bank earnings objectives, require a level of due diligence commensurate with the complexity of the instrument, the materiality of the investment in relation to capital, and the overall quality of the investment portfolio as it relates to serving the liquidity and pledging needs of the bank. The use of traditional credit ratings should be supplemented with the bank's own internal analysis. Bank management should ensure that its valuation process allows for a thorough assessment of projected cash flows and the probability of default and loss given default assumptions.

Failure to adequately diversify investments. Concentrations of investments in the securities of individual obligors or groups of obligors with common economic ties could be an unsound strategy because price fluctuations, a deterioration of the quality of the securities, or loss of principal may adversely affect the bank's financial statements.

Failure to consider pledging requirements in investment decisions.
To meet present and future funding needs, a bank must be able to
pledge eligible securities to support deposits of public funds and to
use as collateral. When developing portfolio and liquidity strategies,
management must consider the eligibility of securities to meet the
bank's pledging and collateral requirements.

**Failure to institute adequate internal controls for investment and
trading activities.** Some banks have experienced substantial losses
because the internal controls on their investment and trading operations
were inadequate to monitor and control risks. A bank with significant
investment portfolio transactions or one engaging in trading activity
should be certain that controls, such as segregation of duties, are in
place.

**Failure to ensure the investment portfolio complies with current
accounting standards.** Current accounting standards require a bank
to divide its investment portfolio into three parts: held-to-maturity,
available-for-sale, and trading. Securities in the held-to-maturity
portfolio are those that a bank has the intent and ability to hold until
maturity. The bank may not use this portfolio to engage in trading
or to conduct speculative securities transactions. The securities in the
available-for-sale account are those that will be sold at a future date but
will not be traded often enough to qualify for the trading account. The
trading portfolio holds securities bought and held principally for selling
in the near term. The bank must record and report trading transactions
in this account.

FIDUCIARY ACTIVITIES

Although traditional personal and employee benefit account
administration remain the primary fiduciary business lines for most
banks, other banks have expanded their fiduciary activities to include
such products and services as investment management accounts, advising
proprietary mutual funds, global custody, and securities lending. Many
large banks have established a private banking department, offering
a full array of credit and investment management services, including
fiduciary services, to high-net-worth individuals. As the fiduciary

business continues to evolve, the wide variety of products and services, frequently offered in locations outside the traditional trust department, presents a complex administrative challenge to bank boards.

Regardless of the scope of the fiduciary activities, however, the board is responsible for monitoring its administration. The board must protect the bank's fiduciary reputation, as well as the customer's assets, by having effective policies and procedures, management information systems, and risk management practices. The board should confirm that individuals who administer fiduciary activities at the bank are knowledgeable and competent, and have high personal integrity. The board should ascertain that internal controls and compliance management systems are adequate to minimize compliance, operational, reputation, and strategic risks associated with fiduciary activities.

FIDUCIARY ACTIVITIES—AREAS OF CONCERN

When considering fiduciary activities, the board should scrutinize the following practices or conditions.

Opening of new accounts not in compliance with account acceptance guidelines. To protect the bank's reputation as a fiduciary, and thereby minimize reputation risk, the bank must know its customers. The board should establish guidelines designed to make sure that only accounts that meet the board's selection standards are accepted. An account acceptance process helps prevent the opening of new accounts with unclear objectives, accounts that management is not qualified to administer, accounts that may lead to conflicts of interest, and accounts that may expose the bank to future liabilities, such as from environmental hazards. The guidelines should specify how exceptions to policy are to be handled and that management should be able to support why an exception should be made.

Purchasing of securities not previously approved by the board or investment committee. The board or investment committee normally establishes investment guidelines and approves investment lists to control the acceptable amount of risk. Any security purchase that falls outside of established guidelines should be carefully evaluated to determine its suitability for an account. Management should document its decision to purchase such an asset.

Higher than anticipated yields on investment portfolios, collective investment funds, or advised mutual funds. Investment managers who are rewarded solely on the performance of the portfolios they manage may have an incentive to accept more risk in order to increase returns. Even if the securities purchased are authorized for the account or fund, the manager may be taking undue risks. For example, a pooled fund may allow investment in mortgage-backed securities. To increase yields, the manager may invest in higher risk mortgage-backed securities or have a concentration of those securities. The board should determine whether the risk assumed to achieve higher than expected returns is acceptable.

Existence of accounts with unusually high cash balances or large or extended overdrafts. A fiduciary is responsible for properly managing fiduciary assets. High cash balances in accounts may indicate that management is failing to meet its responsibility to make fiduciary assets productive. Similarly, large or extended overdrafts may indicate poor management of an account. These situations should be noted on an exception reporting system. The board should expect management to document its reasons for allowing high cash balances or overdrafts.

Failure to institute adequate internal controls for fiduciary activities. Indications that internal controls are weak include references to numerous or repeat exceptions to policies and procedures in internal reports, internal or external audits, or examination reports. To avoid this, the board should approve policies, which management should implement with procedures, establishing a strong internal control structure. The department's organizational structure should provide for separation of duties. Reports noting exceptions to policies should be reviewed on a regular basis, with exceptions properly approved. Significant exceptions should require prior approval by the board or a designated committee.

Losses or settlements arising from actual or threatened litigation that are significant in either size or volume. Losses or settlements may indicate that fiduciary assets are not being administered properly. The board should require management to thoroughly explain any significant losses or litigation and make an effort to identify the cause of the problem. The board should then determine whether the underlying reason for the problem has been corrected. Numerous or increased amounts of customer complaints also may indicate administrative weaknesses. To mitigate reputation and litigation risks, the bank should ensure that all customer complaints are investigated and addressed by management to ensure that customers are being properly served.

Any situations that give rise to a conflict of interest. To protect the bank's reputation as a fiduciary, the board should direct management to implement policies and procedures to avoid conflicts of interest and even the appearance of conflicts. The board should have a review process that checks for compliance with applicable laws, regulations, policies, and procedures. Exceptions should be reported to the board, which should then instruct management to take appropriate corrective action.

INSIDER ACTIVITIES

Public confidence in a bank's operation and condition is fundamental to its ability to attract and maintain deposits at a reasonable cost; a bank must have a reputation for honesty and integrity. Insider abuse ranks high on the list of causes of bank failures and is often the result of a lack of clear written internal policies or a failure to enforce them. The importance of this issue to the very survival of a bank means that the board must assume a leadership role. The board must adopt and enforce strong written insider policies governing the bank's relationship to insiders and their related interests. The board must adopt similar policies to cover bank officers and employees. Failure to control insider activities properly can subject the bank to reputation, strategic, credit, compliance and liquidity risks. Among other things, the board's insider policies should address

☐ Guidelines for insider lending and transactions with bank affiliates.

☐ Disclosure of actual and potential conflicts.

- ☐ Guidelines for handling confidential information.

- ☐ The need for dealings to be at arm's length.

- ☐ Prohibitions against the use of insider information in securities transactions.

- ☐ Prohibitions on self-dealing.

- ☐ Restrictions on the acceptance of gifts, bequests, or other items of value from customers or other persons having a business relationship with the bank.

The board must establish a method to administer and monitor compliance with the bank's insider policies. The board should require management to develop training and awareness programs covering insider issues and should establish lines of communication outside of the normal chain of command. These communication channels, which are intended to increase the likelihood that insiders and employees seek guidance, should provide advice and assistance to directors, officers, and employees as ethics questions arise. The board should monitor questions and responses periodically to ensure consistent interpretations. Finally, the policies should provide clear guidance on what actions the bank will take in the event of noncompliance.

INSIDER ACTIVITIES—AREAS OF CONCERN

In addition to issues discussed elsewhere in this book, such as in the section titled "Loan Portfolio Management—Areas of Concern," the following practices or conditions should trigger additional board scrutiny.

Transactions resulting in a conflict of interest. Bank insiders can and should bring legitimate and profitable business to the bank. Any transaction between a bank and an insider or his or her outside interest, however, should be made in a manner that avoids even the appearance of a conflict of interest. For example, an insider's loans and deposits, and those to his or her interests, should be made on terms and at rates that are comparable with those offered to other customers. Purchases or sales of assets or securities between a bank and its insiders should be made on an arm's-length basis at fair market value. Insiders should disclose their interests and the board should ensure that procedures are in place to closely scrutinize insider transactions. Transactions between the bank and other persons or businesses an insider brings to the bank should be monitored. A bank insider should avoid accepting gifts or soliciting anything of value in connection with any transaction between the bank and its customers.

Payment of excessive compensation or unjustified fees. Insiders who are not bank employees may be entitled to compensation for services they perform for the bank. Compensation can take the form of salaries, bonuses, fees, benefits, or other goods and services. Compensation that is either excessive or contributes to material financial loss to the bank, however, is an unsafe and unsound banking practice and is prohibited by regulatory safety and soundness standards.

Fees paid to insiders for specific services should be based on cost, cost plus a reasonable profit, or current market value. The board should ensure that records are retained that demonstrate the fair value of the goods and services rendered, the benefit to the bank, and the appropriateness of the fees paid. The board should review these records as part of its ongoing supervision of the bank's affairs. If excessive compensation is discovered, the board is responsible for taking corrective action, including seeking restitution.

Failure to comply with laws and regulations. Insider activities are governed by several laws and regulations. They include reporting requirements, limitations on the type and amount of certain insider transactions, approval requirements, and prohibitions on certain types or characteristics of insider transactions. A bank in noncompliance with these laws and regulations may face increased reputation risk and be subject to an administrative action or civil money penalties (CMP). The board should ensure that bank insider policies and procedures incorporate legal requirements and that insiders receive training on these requirements. When complex situations arise, such as the applicability of the various combination and attribution rules for insider lending limits, the bank should seek legal guidance.

IV

THE DIRECTOR'S INDIVIDUAL RESPONSIBILITIES

BE DILIGENT

BE LOYAL TO THE BANK'S INTERESTS

This chapter discusses in practical terms the director's individual responsibilities. The guidance provides common sense advice about how directors can meet these responsibilities when overseeing a bank's operations.

BE DILIGENT

A director of a national bank has distinct individual duties, responsibilities, and potential liabilities. Directors must devote the time and attention necessary to do their jobs. They must be aware of the bank's condition and knowledgeable enough to make meaningful contributions to the board's work. Simply put, a director must diligently and actively perform his or her responsibilities. If not, under some circumstances, individual directors may be held personally liable for losses suffered by the bank or others, or incur other personal liability. While not all-inclusive, the following five points discuss specific actions that a director can take to be diligent.

ATTEND BOARD AND COMMITTEE MEETINGS

Directors who do not attend or participate in board and assigned committee meetings regularly are not fully meeting their responsibilities. Being present at those meetings is important to staying informed about the bank's activities. The OCC considers this duty to be so fundamental that bank examiners may specifically criticize an individual director's unsatisfactory attendance. In addition, the securities laws may require certain banks to publicly disclose a director's poor attendance record. A director's absence from a board meeting, moreover, does not necessarily relieve that director from responsibility for what took place at the meeting. Any director who is unable to attend meetings regularly, because of ill health or other reasons, should consider whether continued membership on the board is in the bank's or the director's best interests.

REQUEST AND REVIEW MEETING MATERIALS

Directors should decide what information they need to stay informed of the bank's condition and to participate meaningfully in board meetings. They are responsible for ensuring that the information selected for review permits the board to fulfill its duties. For its part, management is responsible for providing adequate information to the directors.

Outside directors may benefit from reports specifically tailored to their needs. These directors lack day-to-day exposure to bank activities and should not be expected to monitor operations by receiving extensive, detailed reports on every issue or even the same abbreviated reports prepared for senior management. Instead, outside directors may find reports most useful when they present a current and concise picture of the bank and focus on the issues that demand the board's attention and action.

Directors should ensure that they receive meeting materials early enough to review the information carefully before the meetings. Each director should be familiar with the information provided and should review it carefully and follow up on any questions that the material may raise. The board functions at its best when informed directors interact and apply their individual expertise and varied backgrounds to the decisions facing them.

ASK QUESTIONS AND SEEK EXPLANATIONS OF PROBLEMS

Directors should have a complete and accurate understanding of the bank's condition. If particular matters are unclear, directors should ask management to provide more information. Directors must take the initiative to address potential problems they see. Exceptions from board policies, for instance, should generate directors' inquiries and requests for follow-up information to ensure that proper controls are in place.

Directors can and should feel free to communicate with other directors or management outside of formal board meetings. Both directors and management can benefit from such informal contacts. A director who does not wish to interrupt or ask extensive questions during board meetings might, for instance, find it more convenient and productive to ask questions of management or other directors before or after board meetings. Directors also might find that sitting in on key management planning or review meetings helps them understand issues affecting the bank.

Individual directors should not make decisions before their questions are satisfactorily answered. A director who cannot make an informed decision should ask the board to postpone the decision until adequate information is available or more time is provided for discussion. If this is a recurring problem, the board should review the format of board proceedings or management's responsiveness to inquiries from directors.

UNDERSTAND AUDITS AND SUPERVISORY COMMUNICATIONS

Individual directors should personally review all reports and significant communications from the bank's auditors and regulators and ensure they understand the important issues. Information from such third-party reviews of the bank's operations can help the director, and the entire board, assess the accuracy and validity of information from management. A director who wants help understanding the findings or recommendations of a report can contact the bank's audit committee or the examiners, auditors, or outside consultants who prepared the report.

Regulatory and other third-party reports, such as outside audit reports, also provide notice to directors of problems in the bank. These reports may show that losses from uncorrected problem areas resulted from the board's failure to supervise the bank adequately. Because of the significance of these reports and the fact that bank regulators may hold individual directors accountable, directors should understand the problems identified and ensure that management takes needed corrective actions within specified time frames.

EXERCISE INDEPENDENT JUDGMENT

Directors should be objective and independent when overseeing the bank's affairs. Each director should examine and consider management's recommendations thoroughly. Examples of situations in which a director could feel uncomfortable exercising independent judgment include

☐ Inside directors who may feel a need to support management actions to keep their jobs.

☐ Inside directors who may have a biased judgment because of their involvement in specific bank operations.

☐ Outside directors who may believe that they do not know enough about banking to meaningfully evaluate management's recommendations.

☐ Outside directors who were invited by the CEO to join the board and may feel pressure to support management if they wish to remain directors.

☐ Both inside and outside directors who may feel compelled to vote with a controlling shareholder (who is also a director) to keep their positions.

Despite these fears, pressures, and concerns, individual directors must exercise independent judgment. Directors should ask management the questions and elicit the facts necessary to satisfy themselves that management's recommendations are feasible and in the bank's best interests.

Each director contributes an important perspective to the board. The exercise of objective judgment is critical to the board's effectiveness. If a director disagrees with a board action on the basis of his or her own review of the matter, the director should state formally his or her view, explain the reasons for disagreement, and request that the position be recorded in the board minutes. Thoughtful disagreement among directors is healthy and can suggest that the board is independent and not operating under undue influence by management or from an individual director. A director's recorded dissent in the board minutes also may protect that director from some potential liability resulting from the board action.

BE LOYAL TO THE BANK'S INTERESTS

Directors are responsible for dealing fairly with the bank in business transactions and for ensuring that their personal interests do not bias board decisions or otherwise harm the bank. While transactions between a bank and its directors may be important to the bank, directors must ensure that their own business and personal relationships with the bank, and the bank's relationship with the other directors, are always at arm's length.

Also, directors must not improperly take business opportunities away from the bank. Although the law does not prohibit a bank director from doing business with the bank, directors must ensure that they do not abuse their position to benefit personally at the bank's expense. Directors must structure their business and personal dealings with the bank to comply with legal requirements and to avoid even the appearance of a conflict of interest. In addition, directors must take reasonable action to prevent other employees from abusing their positions with the bank.

Insider activities can lead to reputation, liquidity, compliance, and credit risks. If a director does not carefully follow insider laws and regulations, the bank's reputation and that of its directors may be tarnished. If these problems become known to the public, the bank may experience liquidity problems and compliance risk may increase. The bank may be exposed to credit risk when insiders use their positions to obtain loans for which they or other borrowers might not otherwise qualify.

Directors must approve written insider policies for the bank that address codes of conduct, conflicts of interest, and other relevant issues. Insider policies, including codes of conduct, address the activities of directors, officers, and employees at all levels of the bank. An appropriate code of conduct can set a pattern for proper behavior by directors and all bank employees and help avoid future supervisory and legal problems. Directors and other insiders can conduct business with the bank according to an established routine that recognizes and observes all of the policies' requirements. Moreover, following these policies should make compliance with the legal restrictions on insider dealings easier.

After approving written insider policies for the bank as a whole, directors should have processes for handling insider transactions. Individual directors can avoid illegal insider transactions in many ways by

☐ Following written insider policies, including a reasonable, judicious bank policy on directors' salaries, fees, loans, and expenses.

☐ Consulting with bank or personal legal counsel before entering into or approving transactions involving the bank and a director or a company controlled by a director.

☐ Disclosing all real or potential conflicts to the entire board before a board decision is made. For example, a director should disclose any ownership interest in or other personal or business relationship to a borrowing entity before a loan is discussed or approved; in some instances, prior disclosure is required by law and regulation.

☐ Making sure that transactions between the bank and a director or company controlled by that director are documented fully. Documentation for such transactions might include:

— Independent appraisals of property that the bank is considering buying, leasing, or selling from or to a director, or other documents establishing the competitiveness of the terms.

— Information showing that a proposed loan to a director or his or her business interest is comparable with specific loans made by the bank to non-insiders.

— Information showing that a proposed loan to a director or his or her business interest does not involve more than the normal risk of repayment or present other unfavorable features.

— Board minutes that reflect the nature of the board's deliberations regarding a potential conflict of interest involving a director.

— Board actions approving such transactions, consistent with applicable legal and regulatory requirements.

- ☐ Making sure that a director with a potential conflict of interest in any matter refrains from discussing, voting, or having any other involvement in the matter. Whether the matter requires board approval or not, the director should disclose all the facts relevant to the transaction and his or her potential conflict and ensure that this action is documented, preferably in the board minutes. When directors engage in a transaction with the bank or a third party, they are required to disclose all information about the matter that is material to the bank, even if the information is confidential.

- ☐ Observing the rule that the bank's interests must be paramount in any transaction involving a director or a company controlled by a director.

V

DIRECTORS AND THE LAW

FIDUCIARY DUTIES AND RESPONSIBILITIES

STATUTORY AND REGULATORY LIABILITY

INDEMNIFICATION AND INSURANCE

When directors are appointed or elected, they are required to take an oath under Federal Banking Law 12 USC 73. The oath states that they will, so far as the duty devolves on them, diligently and honestly administer the affairs of such association and will not knowingly violate or willingly permit to be violated any provisions of banking law. This chapter discusses how the duties referred to in 12 USC 73 have come to be commonly defined and includes practical examples. The chapter also summarizes key banking and other laws and regulations under which a director may face liability. The chapter concludes with a brief discussion of the law as it relates to indemnification and insurance agreements.

FIDUCIARY DUTIES AND RESPONSIBILITIES

The duties of care and loyalty, and good faith, are the standards that guide all actions that directors take. By fully understanding these fiduciary standards and putting the liability environment into proper perspective, directors can perform their duties more effectively. Directors with such understanding are then empowered to take reasonable business risks to preserve and enhance shareholder value, while at the same time prudently managing their own personal liability risks.

These fiduciary duties generally require that

☐ A bank director diligently and honestly administer the bank's affairs.

☐ A bank director place the bank's interests above his or her own interests.

□ Any transactions between a director and the bank be conducted on terms that are fair to the bank.

□ A bank director may authorize bank management to take only those actions or perform only those activities that are legally permitted for the bank.

The **duty of care** requires that directors act in good faith, with the level of care that an ordinarily prudent person would exercise in similar circumstances, and in a manner that they reasonably believe is in the best interests of the organization. The duty of care requires directors to acquire sufficient knowledge of the material facts related to the proposed transaction, thoroughly examine all information available to them with a critical eye, and actively participate in the decision-making process.

The **duty of loyalty** requires that directors exercise their powers in the interests of the organization and its stockholders rather than in the director's own self-interest or in the interests of any other person. Directors taking action on a particular item must be independent, meaning they can consider the transaction on its merits, free from any extraneous influences. The duty of loyalty primarily relates to conflicts of interest, confidentiality, and corporate opportunity.

The duty of loyalty does not mean that a director may not do business with the bank or may not participate in transactions in which the bank may have an interest. However, it does mean that a director must disclose fully to the board any personal interest that he or she has in matters affecting the bank and must also disclose all material, nonprivileged information relevant to the matter. Independent and disinterested directors must decide that any transactions involving these interests are fair to the bank.

A group of directors offers to lease property or equipment to their bank. To avoid breaching the duty of loyalty, the directors must advise the board of their specific interest in the matter and of any material information relevant to the transaction. The disinterested directors must then decide independently that the transaction is fair to the bank because the terms are at least as favorable as those available from other persons or entities unaffiliated with the bank. To make this decision, disinterested directors may, for example, obtain independent appraisals and bids to be sure their deliberations are impartial and that they independently analyzed all relevant information.

A director discovers that property the bank has been considering acquiring for a branch is for sale. The director wants to buy the property personally. The director may avoid liability under the usurpation of corporate opportunity doctrine if he or she allows the bank the first opportunity to purchase the property. If the bank decides against purchasing the property after disinterested directors have fairly and fully considered the facts, the interested director may pursue the matter or recommend it to others.

Under the **business judgment rule,** a court may presume that directors have made decisions on an informed basis, in good faith, and in the honest belief that the action was taken in the best interests of the corporation. This presumption offers directors protection where the courts decline to second-guess their decisions based on a showing that directors followed their duties of care and loyalty, and acted in good faith.

These fiduciary standards focus on such cultural characteristics as independence, objectivity, candor, good faith, diligence, attention, engagement, and integrity. Directors who understand the importance of establishing the right tone at the top better exemplify the conduct and behaviors that enable them to fulfill their responsibilities. They have a clearer idea of the importance of corporate culture and a deeper understanding of their fiduciary responsibilities under the law. They are able to focus not only on process but also on substance— the achievement of sound business strategy and the enhancement of shareholder value.

Each director should take care to ensure that his or her conduct reflects the level of care and diligence required of national bank directors. A national bank director—like the director of any other corporate entity—may be held personally liable in lawsuits for losses resulting from his or her breach of fiduciary duties. Parties including shareholders (either individually or on behalf of the bank), depositors, or creditors who allege injury by a director's failure to fulfill these duties may bring such suits. In addition, the OCC may assess CMPs or take other enforcement action against directors for breaches of fiduciary duty. Potential director liability may be assessed on an individual basis because the nature of any breach in fiduciary duty can vary for each director.

STATUTORY AND REGULATORY LIABILITY

Various statutes and regulations incorporate the concept of the director's duty of care and duty of loyalty. These statutes and regulations set out specific terms for the conduct and activities of directors and their banks.

A director who violates any banking law or regulation, engages in an unsafe or unsound banking practice, or breaches a fiduciary duty (or permits another person to do so) may be held personally liable or subjected to monetary penalties or other sanctions. The director may be held responsible either alone or jointly with other board members or related interests of the director in lawsuits or in administrative actions.

Two directors are aware that an officer of the bank is authorizing repeated overdrafts and loans that exceed the bank's legal lending limit. Although the officer's actions are illegal and subject the bank to substantial credit risk, the two directors take no steps to prevent the offending officer from continuing the practices and decide not to inform the board of the problem. The two directors' inaction enables the officer to continue these practices, which result in significant losses to the bank. The two directors' failure to take appropriate action to stop the practices and alert the rest of the board of the officer's conduct represents a disregard for the bank's safety and soundness and could subject them to a lawsuit or an administrative action. In addition, an administrative action may be brought against the officer who engaged in the improper conduct.

KEY BANKING LAW PROVISIONS

Directors are responsible for ensuring that the bank complies with all applicable laws and regulations. These laws and regulations cover a wide range of banking issues, such as general corporate structure and governance, bank assets, bank operating authorities, and consumer protection. Directors might find it helpful for in-house or outside counsel to periodically review the broad statutory and regulatory framework, brief the board on statutory or regulatory developments particularly relevant to their bank's activities, and advise the directors on specific compliance issues that may arise.

Listed below are some statutes and related regulations that merit special attention because they are often relevant to transactions engaged in by a bank. The descriptions of these statutes and regulations are not intended to be authoritative restatements of the law and regulations, particularly since statutory and regulatory changes may take place after this book is published. Directors and management are responsible for consulting the current version of the specific statutes and regulations implicated by a particular transaction or consulting legal counsel as appropriate. The statutes and regulations involve the following topics:

- ☐ Corporate governance

- ☐ Lending limits

- ☐ Insider transactions

- ☐ Transactions with affiliates

- ☐ Safe and sound banking practices

- ☐ Reporting requirements

- ☐ Other laws and regulations

CORPORATE GOVERNANCE
(SARBANES-OXLEY ACT OF 2002, 12 CFR 363)

The Sarbanes-Oxley Act addresses external auditors and audits, financial reporting and disclosures, conflicts of interest, audit committees, and other corporate governance issues at public companies. A public company is defined as a company that has a class of registered securities with the SEC or the appropriate federal banking agency under Section 12 of the Securities and Exchange Act of 1934.

The FDIC's Part 363 applies to both public and nonpublic banks and holding companies having $500 million or more in total assets. Part 363 establishes requirements for independent financial statement audits; timing, content, and types of management and auditor reporting; and audit committee structure and responsibilities. In addition, all national banks subject to Part 363 are expected to comply with the Sarbanes-Oxley Act's auditor independence provisions and any SEC regulations issued that relate to that section.

LENDING LIMITS (12 USC 84, 12 CFR 32)

The law limits the total dollar amount a bank can lend[13] to a single borrower (including any bank insider or employee). Congress imposed these limits to restrict the impact of a default by any individual borrower on the overall safety and soundness of a bank. The limits are also intended to promote credit diversification among a broad range of borrowers.

A bank computes the dollar amount of the lending limit as a percentage of its capital and surplus. A bank must recalculate its lending limit quarterly when it files its call report, basing the new calculation on the amount of the bank's capital and surplus at the end of the previous quarter. In special circumstances, such as a merger or in the event of a major adverse change in a bank's financial condition, the OCC can send a written notice to a bank requiring it to calculate its limit more frequently. Also, a bank must recalculate immediately its lending limit any time its capital category changes under the OCC's prompt corrective action regulation.

---

[13] Effective one year after the transfer date, the Dodd-Frank Wall Street Reform and Consumer Protection Act amends the lending-limit definition of loans and extensions of credit to include any credit exposure to a person arising from a derivative transaction, repurchase agreement, reverse repurchase agreement, securities lending transaction, or securities borrowing transaction between the bank and the person.

In addition, the OCC's lending-limit rules require that loans to separate but related borrowers be aggregated and attributed to one or more borrowers under specified circumstances, including when apparently separate borrowers in fact constitute a "common enterprise" or when one borrower receives a direct benefit as a result of a loan made to another borrower. Bank management must therefore review carefully all relevant facts and circumstances, including the purpose of the loan and the ultimate recipient of the proceeds, to determine whether combination or attribution is warranted.

A bank makes a loan to an officer of a corporate borrower. The corporate borrower already has two earlier loans from the bank. The officer obtains the new loan in his or her own name, disclosing that it is for the purpose of covering the corporation's overdraft, and deposits the loan proceeds directly into the corporate checking account with the bank. Although the bank makes the loan in the officer's name, the bank must attribute the loan to the corporate borrower and combine it with the corporation's other two loans because the proceeds of the individual's loans are used to benefit the corporation.

Before personally approving a loan, a director should always know, and should make sure that management knows, the applicable loan limit and the total debt to the bank attributable to the borrower. Legal counsel can be helpful in analyzing complex lending-limit questions. A director should be certain that the bank has systems for monitoring the bank's current dollar loan limits and borrowers' loan balances so that a loan is not approved in excess of the lending limits. Those systems should be adequate to alert management to loans made to separate but related borrowers that must be combined or attributed under the law. When bank officers or directors decide that loans to related borrowers need not be combined under the lending-limit rules, they should document their decision and supporting rationale in the credit file.

INSIDER TRANSACTIONS
(12 USC 375, 375a, 375b, 1972; 12 CFR 31, 215)[14]

Federal laws and regulations impose qualitative and quantitative limitations on a bank's ability to make loans[15] to its "insiders" (directors, executive officers, and principal shareholders and their respective related interests—usually companies controlled by these insiders). These laws and regulations are designed to prevent misuse of depositors' funds and to avoid potential conflicts of interest. Because the statutory and regulatory restrictions on insider transactions do not apply uniformly to all insiders, the board must become familiar with them and pay careful attention to whom a particular restriction applies. In addition, as with lending limits, certain loans to insiders require aggregation or attribution with loans to certain of their related interests.

Insider transaction laws impose dollar limits on a bank's ability to provide loans to individual insiders, just as they impose dollar limits on loans to borrowers unaffiliated with the bank. One of the key federal insider lending-limit statutes expressly incorporates the dollar limits contained in 12 USC 84 (the national bank lending limit statute) and applies them to insiders. Some, but not all exceptions to the lending limits contained in 12 USC 84 and 12 CFR 32 (the OCC regulation that implements the lending-limit statute) are also available for loans to insiders.

Executive officers of the bank itself (but not of the bank's affiliates) are subject to some additional restrictions not applicable to other insiders. Broadly stated, these additional restrictions allow the bank to extend the following loans only if the executive officer has submitted a detailed, current financial statement; if the loans are reported to the board in a timely manner; and if the loans are not on preferential terms:

---

[14] Effective on the transfer date, 12 USC 375 is repealed by the Dodd-Frank Wall Street Reform and Consumer Protection Act and replaced with a new provision, 12 USC 1828(z). See footnote 15.

[15] Effective one year after the transfer date, the Dodd-Frank Wall Street Reform and Consumer Protection Act amends 12 USC 375b to provide that a bank extends credit to a person by having credit exposure to the person arising from a derivative transaction (as defined in the national bank lending limit), repurchase agreement, reverse repurchase agreement, securities lending transaction, or securities borrowing transaction between the member bank and the person.

- A loan in any amount up to the bank's general lending limit for the purchase of a residence.

- A loan in any amount up to the bank's general lending limit for the education of the executive officer's children.

- A loan for any other purpose(s) up to the limit prescribed by regulation (currently $100,000 for most banks).

When the aggregate amount of all loans outstanding to any individual insider reaches a certain limit, a majority of the disinterested directors must approve in advance any additional amount loaned to that insider. Federal law also imposes a separate limit on the dollar amount of loans that a bank can make to all of its insiders as a group. As is the case with loans to executive officers, some, but not all, of the exceptions contained in 12 USC 84 and 12 CFR 32 are available for the group lending limits.

Insider transaction laws also prohibit all insiders who transact business with their bank from receiving preferential treatment. Generally, the bank must conduct such transactions on terms comparable with those available to bank customers who are not insiders or employees of the bank. For example, a bank may not make a loan to a bank director at a lower interest rate or on other more favorable terms (such as waiving points on a mortgage loan) than loans provided to other customers in similar circumstances. Other prohibitions on loans to insiders include

- Making a loan to an insider without applying the bank's normal credit underwriting procedures.

- Making an insider loan when the loan carries a greater than normal risk of repayment.

- Failing to require the same type and amount of collateral that the bank requires of borrowers who are not insiders or bank employees.

The laws governing insider transactions also specifically prohibit banks from paying overdrafts on a director's or executive officer's account unless the overdraft is small (less than $1,000), short in duration (less than five days), and inadvertent, or payment has been preauthorized in writing according to regulatory requirements.

> *A $5,000 check drawn on a director's account, which has a balance of only $3,000, is presented for payment at the director's bank.* The bank tries to reach the director to advise him or her of the problem and discovers that the director is out of the country for the next 10 days and is unavailable to cover the check. The director has not established an approved overdraft plan with the bank. As a result, the bank may not cover the check.

Other insider transaction limitations prohibit a bank from selling to or purchasing from its directors securities or other assets on preferential terms unless the transaction has received prior approval from a majority of the bank's disinterested directors.[16] Before granting this approval, they must determine that such a transaction is consistent with safe and sound banking practices and with the directors' fiduciary duties.

TRANSACTIONS WITH AFFILIATES
(12 USC 371c, 371c-1; 12 CFR 223)

Shifting resources among bank affiliates, including those within a holding company structure, may be expedient. Such transactions, however, can sometimes strengthen an affiliate at the expense of its affiliate bank. Congress enacted statutory safeguards to prevent banks and their subsidiaries from being abused or disadvantaged by transactions with affiliated entities.

These statutory provisions limit specified transactions with affiliates to a percentage of the bank's capital and surplus. Transactions covered include loans to an affiliate; purchases of assets from or securities issued by an affiliate; the acceptance of an affiliate's securities as collateral for a loan to a third party; and the issuance of a guarantee, acceptance, or letter of credit on behalf of an affiliate.[17]

---

[16] Effective on the transfer date, the Dodd-Frank Wall Street Reform and Consumer Protection Act imposes a stricter requirement under which a bank is prohibited from purchasing an asset from or selling an asset to an insider, unless the transaction is on market terms and, if the transaction exceeds 10 percent of the bank's capital stock and surplus, it is approved in advance by a majority of disinterested directors.

[17] Effective one year after the transfer date, the Dodd-Frank Wall Street Reform and Consumer Protection Act amends 12 USC 371c and 371c-1 inter alia to expand the transactions covered to include a transaction with an affiliate that involves the borrowing or lending of securities, and a derivative transaction (as defined in the national bank lending limit) with an affiliate, in each case to the extent that the transaction causes a member bank or a subsidiary to have credit exposure to the affiliate.

Additional nonquantitative restrictions apply as well. For example, loans to an affiliate must be properly secured according to a formula specified by statute. No bank may make a loan to an affiliate if that loan is secured by that or any other affiliate's securities. The law prohibits a national bank from purchasing from an affiliate low-quality assets, such as loans in a nonaccrual status, loans on which principal and interest are more than 30 days past due, loans classified or treated as "special mention" in the most recent report of examination or inspection, or loans whose terms have been renegotiated due to deteriorating financial condition.

To comply with these restrictions, directors should make sure that the bank independently evaluates the quality of an asset before it is purchased from an affiliate. Directors should ask bank management whether assets purchased from affiliates meet statutory standards. They should be aware that all transactions with affiliates must be at arm's length; no preferential terms may be offered.

SAFE AND SOUND BANKING PRACTICES (12 CFR 30)

A director must oversee the bank's compliance with safe and sound banking practices. A practice that is unsafe and unsound is any practice or conduct that is contrary to generally accepted standards for prudent bank operations and that, if continued, might result in abnormal risk of loss or damage to the bank, its shareholders, or the federal deposit insurance fund.

Certain safety and soundness standards are detailed in 12 CFR 30. These standards provide banks with broad guidance to follow when establishing their own practices. In 12 CFR 30, the following general areas of bank operations are covered:

☐ Operational and managerial standards, including

— Internal controls and information systems.

— Internal audit system.

— Loan documentation.

— Credit underwriting.

— Interest rate exposure.

— Asset growth.

— Asset quality.

— Earnings.

— Compensation, fees, and benefits.

☐ Information security standards.

☐ Standards for residential mortgage lending practices.

REPORTING REQUIREMENTS (12 USC 161)

The law requires banks to submit a Report of Condition and Income (call report) on a quarterly basis. These call reports, which are public documents, along with other publicly available material about the bank, enable individuals engaged in or considering doing business with a bank to make informed decisions about the condition of that bank. The OCC may impose other reporting requirements on national banks to help the agency monitor the condition of banks.

The information a bank submits in a call report must be accurate. The report must be signed by the bank's chief financial officer, and three directors must attest to the report's correctness.

A bank that inaccurately represents its condition in its call reports may be breaching its reporting responsibilities and be subject to penalties. Directors who attest to the accuracy of such reports may also be subject to penalties or other administrative action. Similar inaccurate disclosures in other bank documents also may violate the reporting and antifraud provisions of the federal securities laws.

OTHER LAWS AND REGULATIONS

SECURITIES LAWS (15 USC 77a, 78a)

Directors who make material misrepresentations or omissions or act upon material nonpublic information or otherwise engage in fraudulent conduct in connection with the purchase or sale of securities may be liable for violations of the securities laws and therefore subject to penalties. Investors, the OCC, and the SEC may bring an action against a director for fraudulent conduct under the antifraud provisions of the securities laws. A director may be liable for fraud in a securities transaction, depending on the nature of the director's involvement in, and knowledge of, the transaction. Directors who purchase or sell securities on the basis of nonpublic confidential information to profit or avoid loss at the expense of other investors may be liable for insider trading under the antifraud provisions. Directors who engage in activity that violates state antifraud statutes governing intrastate sales of securities may be subject to liability under state law.

When a national bank issues securities, it is subject to regulations that are designed to protect the bank's capital and its investors. The OCC's regulations incorporate by reference certain SEC regulations and generally require the bank to prepare and file with the OCC an accurate and complete offering statement that gives public investors all the information they need to make an informed investment decision. The OCC may require a bank to correct or rescind an offering circular that does not disclose adequate and complete information. Directors responsible for material misrepresentations or omissions in an offering circular may be subject to liability under the antifraud provisions.

Any national bank with 500 or more shareholders at the end of a fiscal year and assets exceeding $5 million must register its equity securities with the OCC. Banks that meet these requirements are often referred to as "registered" banks. Registered banks must comply with certain reporting and disclosure requirements under the federal securities laws, including the Sarbanes-Oxley Act. For example, directors are responsible for reporting changes in ownership of bank stock. A director may be liable in an action brought by the OCC, the SEC, or injured investors for a bank's failure to comply with these requirements.

ANTITRUST LAWS (12 USC 1828(c), 15 USC 1, 2, 18)

Banks are subject to both generally applicable antitrust laws and antitrust laws that apply specifically to banks. Generally applicable antitrust laws prohibit banks from undertaking actions in restraint of trade, such as fixing interest rates or fees, allocating markets between competitors, or monopolizing a market.

Other antitrust laws and regulations apply specifically to banks, including those imposing restrictions on mergers and other types of business combinations. Antitrust regulations prohibit bank mergers that will substantially lessen competition. A merger that would be in restraint of trade also is prohibited, such as a merger whose sole purpose is to eliminate a competitor. Two other antitrust laws that specifically apply to banks cover management interlocks and antitying issues.

MANAGEMENT INTERLOCKS (12 USC 3201, 12 CFR 26)

Laws and regulations regarding management interlocks generally prevent officials of one depository institution from being involved in the management of another depository institution in the same area or, in larger depository institutions, no matter where the institutions are located. Certain exceptions apply, however, such as in troubled institutions or institutions doing business outside the United States.

ANTITYING (12 USC 1972)

Broadly stated, banks are generally prohibited from extending credit, leasing or selling property, furnishing services, or varying prices if they impose a condition that the customer either (1) obtain another product or service from the bank or any of its affiliates or (2) not obtain an additional product or service from a competitor. For example, antitying provisions prohibit

☐ The extension of credit or a reduction in the price of credit on the condition that a customer purchase "other real estate owned" from the bank.

☐ The sale of property to a customer on the condition or requirement that the customer obtain securities services from an affiliate.

☐ The extension of credit to a customer on the condition that the customer not obtain a loan from a competitor (unless the restriction ensures the soundness of the credit).

☐ The provision of a letter of credit to a customer on the condition that the customer lease space to the bank at a favorable rate.

Certain transactions are not subject to these antitying prohibitions. For example, a bank may rely on a "traditional bank products" exception to require that a customer obtain a loan, discount, deposit, or trust service in order to be eligible to obtain some other products offered by the bank. Likewise, a bank can vary charges on traditional bank products or brokerage services if the customer obtains a traditional bank product from an affiliate.

CRIMINAL LAWS (18 USC 215, 656, 1001, 1005, 1344)

A national bank director may be criminally liable for his or her actions as a director. For example, directors may incur criminal liability if they

☐ Falsify bank records.

☐ Misuse or misapply bank funds or assets.

☐ Request or accept fees or gifts to influence, or as a reward for, bank business.

☐ Make false statements generally.

In addition, criminal laws require national banks to report suspected criminal violations to the OCC and to federal law enforcement agencies. The OCC also refers suspected criminal activity in national banks to law enforcement officials. If a suspected criminal activity leads to a criminal conviction, a plea agreement, or a pretrial diversion program (first-time offenders program to avoid prosecution by performing community service), and the criminal offense involves dishonesty or breach of trust, the person may not serve as a director, officer, employee, or institution-affiliated party (IAP)[18] of any FDIC-insured bank unless the FDIC provides specific consent.

---

[18] In addition to directors, IAPs include bank officers, employees, controlling stockholders, and other individuals who participate in the affairs of the bank.

INDEMNIFICATION AND INSURANCE

A bank director may not be able to avoid being named as a defendant in lawsuits challenging the business decisions and activities of board members. A director can, however, obtain some protection against large financial losses through indemnification agreements and insurance. An indemnification agreement, which is included in the bank's bylaws if adopted, specifies that the bank will reimburse a director for expenses incurred in legal actions when the director was performing services for the bank. Such agreements should be consistent with safe and sound banking practices. The bank also may provide insurance protection for a director, generally in the form of director and officer liability insurance. If a director has breached his or her fiduciary duties to the bank, however, any indemnification agreement may be void.

National banks are subject to regulations governing indemnification. For example, indemnification provisions that apply to administrative proceedings or civil actions initiated by a federal banking agency must be reasonable and consistent with the requirements of 12 USC 1828(k) and its implementing regulations. In addition, national banks may purchase insurance for expenses covered by indemnification provisions but may not purchase insurance to pay CMP assessments imposed by a bank regulatory authority.

Fidelity bond coverage is appropriate for all banks because it insures risks that contain the potential for significant loss. The failure of directors to require bonds with adequate sureties and in sufficient amounts may make them personally liable for any losses the bank sustains because of the absence of such bonds.

VI

ADMINISTRATIVE ACTIONS

ACTIONS AGAINST NATIONAL BANKS
ACTIONS AGAINST INDIVIDUALS

Previous chapters of this book described matters that a board of directors of any national bank should understand to help the bank operate soundly. This chapter deals with the types of remedies available to the OCC to address problems in a bank or with its directors. These remedies are designed primarily to help a bank overcome deficiencies in its operations.

Because the OCC and a bank's directors and management have a mutual interest in improving the condition of a bank in which problems have been identified, it is in both parties' best interests to take corrective action promptly. The OCC decides on a case-by-case basis whether to bring an action against a bank or a director or other IAP and the nature and extent of the action. The OCC considers how best to correct violations and unsafe and unsound banking practices and to prevent future bank problems. Key factors in the OCC's decision-making process include

☐ The seriousness of the problems or the violations of law.

☐ The board's history of cooperation with the OCC and the apparent ability and willingness of the board to take the appropriate corrective actions.

The examiner's exit meeting with bank management may be the bank's first indication that the OCC has concerns about the bank and is considering an administrative action. Directors may attend this meeting and should use this opportunity to seek advice about how to correct existing or potential problems.

Directors also may request a meeting with other OCC personnel (such as supervisory office and legal staff) if the OCC has indicated that it is considering an administrative action. OCC personnel will discuss the reasons for the proposed action as well as the specific problems that need to be addressed.

A national bank can appeal any dispute concerning the examination findings to its OCC supervisory Deputy Comptroller or the OCC Ombudsman before the administrative process begins. The period between the end of an examination and the time the findings are formalized in a report of examination provides a good opportunity for the bank to formulate and begin to carry out a reasonable plan to correct problems that examiners noted. The actions that the board proposes to deal with these concerns should be documented in the board minutes. In addition, the OCC encourages, and under certain circumstances requires, banks to submit responses stating the bank's commitment to a corrective plan and specifying the terms of the plan. During this period, the bank is encouraged to stay in contact with its OCC supervisory office and to work with the OCC to respond promptly and positively to the agency's concerns.

Good-faith discussions between the board and the OCC generally are successful in bringing about a speedy and mutually acceptable resolution of differences. These discussions should focus on devising a realistic and reasonable method to restore the bank to a safe and sound condition. Failure to correct cited problems promptly and decisively can result in more severe OCC action.

ACTIONS AGAINST NATIONAL BANKS

The OCC may choose to take actions to correct specific problems identified at a bank. Actions typically specify what the bank needs to do to correct identified problems, such as improving lending practices, raising capital, instituting proper policies and procedures, or correcting specific violations of law. These actions may take the form of an informal or formal enforcement action. The OCC also may assess CMPs against a bank or, under certain extreme situations, place a bank into conservatorship or receivership.

The OCC places an enforcement action on a bank after obtaining the consent of a majority of the bank's directors about the remedies to correct problems. If the OCC does not receive such consent, it may begin an administrative proceeding to impose one of the more formal actions. The OCC has the authority under Prompt Corrective Action to impose certain requirements on a bank in the absence of consent and without the normal administrative process. Whether the administrative action is entered into by consent or imposed through an administrative proceeding, all directors are ultimately responsible for the bank's compliance with the action. Enforcement actions, with the exception of temporary cease-and-desist orders, remain in effect until the OCC determines that the bank's overall condition has improved significantly and the bank has achieved sustained compliance with the terms of the document. When this occurs, the OCC may terminate the enforcement action.

INFORMAL ENFORCEMENT ACTIONS

COMMITMENT LETTER

A commitment letter is a document signed by the bank's board of directors on behalf of the bank and acknowledged by an authorized OCC official, reflecting specific written commitments to take corrective actions in response to problems or concerns identified by the OCC in its supervision of the bank. The document may be drafted by either the OCC or the bank. A commitment letter is not a binding legal document. Failure to honor the commitments, however, provides strong evidence of the need for formal action.

MEMORANDUM OF UNDERSTANDING

A memorandum of understanding (MOU) is a bilateral document signed by the bank's board of directors on behalf of the bank and an authorized OCC representative. An MOU is drafted by the OCC and in form and content looks very much like a formal OCC enforcement action. An MOU legally has the same force and effect as a commitment letter.

Under 12 USC 1831p-1 and 12 CFR 30, the OCC issues to the bank a determination and notification of failure to meet safety and soundness standards and requires the submission of a safety and soundness compliance plan (collectively called a Notice of Deficiency). At a minimum, the plan must include a description of the steps the bank will take to correct the deficiencies and the time within which these steps are to be taken. If the safety and soundness plan is approved, the plan functions as an informal enforcement action. However, if the bank fails to submit an acceptable safety and soundness plan or fails, in any material respect, to implement an approved plan, the OCC must, by order (see Safety and Soundness Order under Formal Enforcement Actions), require the bank to correct the deficiencies. The OCC may, by order, require the bank to take any other action that the OCC determines will better carry out the purposes of 12 USC 1831p-1.

FORMAL ENFORCEMENT ACTIONS

FORMAL AGREEMENT

A formal agreement is similar in form to an MOU. Like an MOU and a commitment letter, a formal agreement requires agreement between the OCC and the bank about the action necessary to correct the identified problems. A formal agreement is proposed when the problems in the bank are not too severe and management is cooperative. A formal agreement differs from an MOU and a commitment letter, however, in that a formal agreement is a public document and the OCC may assess CMPs for any violation of that agreement. In addition, the OCC may order compliance with a formal agreement through a cease-and-desist order.

ORDERS UNDER 12 USC 1818

Through the use of a cease-and-desist order (C&D), the OCC may fashion appropriate remedies for violations of law or unsafe or unsound banking practices. The OCC may use a C&D to require banks to stop certain practices and to take affirmative action to correct conditions resulting from the violations or practices at issue. C&Ds are issued most often when the agency is not confident that bank management has the ability and willingness to take the necessary corrective action or when the problems are so severe that a lesser action cannot be justified.

When the OCC determines that a C&D is required, the agency brings the problems to the directors' attention and presents the directors with an order specifying the necessary corrective actions. Usually, the OCC presents the order at a board meeting. At that time, the OCC asks for the board's consent to the order. Consent order is the title given by the OCC to a C&D that is entered into and becomes final through the board of directors' execution on behalf of the bank of a Stipulation and Consent document. Once an order becomes effective, all directors are responsible for compliance with it. A C&D remains in effect until the OCC terminates it.

If consent to a C&D is not obtained, the OCC may decide to serve a notice of charges setting forth the basis for the action. A notice of charges typically is a public document. The bank must file an answer to the charges contained in the notice, after which the matter proceeds to a formal administrative hearing.

The Administrative Procedure Act specifies that an administrative hearing is to be held on the charges before an independent administrative law judge (ALJ). The hearing typically is open to the public, and the OCC has the burden of proving the charges in the notice of charges by a preponderance of the evidence. After the hearing and the filing of briefs by counsel, the ALJ files a recommended decision. The Comptroller of the Currency then reviews the entire case, with the assistance of agency counsel who have had no involvement with the administrative action, and renders a final agency decision. If the Comptroller's decision is adverse to the bank and results in the issuance of a C&D, the bank can appeal the case to a U.S. Court of Appeals.

If a bank fails to comply with a C&D, the OCC may take the matter to federal district court to seek a mandatory injunction requiring compliance with a C&D. If the injunction is not obeyed, contempt of court proceedings may be pursued. Moreover, a willful violation of a final C&D is itself grounds for receivership, and violation of substantial safety and soundness articles in a C&D can help establish the unsafe or unsound practices or condition that is an element of several other receivership grounds. The OCC also has the authority to impose CMPs or take other administrative action against any individual officer, director, or other IAP who, directly or indirectly, engaged in or participated in the violation.

The OCC may issue a temporary C&D before a cease-and-desist proceeding is completed. This may occur when the OCC determines that such immediate action is necessary to protect the bank and when the alleged misconduct, or its continuation, would likely cause the bank to become insolvent, cause a significant dissipation of bank assets or earnings, weaken the bank's condition, or prejudice the interests of the depositors. The OCC also may issue a temporary C&D if a bank's books and records are so incomplete or inaccurate that the agency cannot determine the financial condition of the bank or the details or purpose of any material transaction through the normal supervisory process. A temporary C&D may require the bank to cease and desist from the violation or practice or to take affirmative corrective action. A bank has 10 days to appeal a temporary C&D to a federal district court. A temporary C&D, however, is effective upon service and remains in effect until the administrative proceedings concerning the C&D are complete, unless it is set aside by court order or the OCC terminates the order.

CAPITAL DIRECTIVE

Minimum capital requirements are established for all national banks by regulation. When appropriate, the OCC may establish higher capital requirements for a particular bank. Unless there are immediate time constraints, the OCC gives a bank notice and opportunity to comment on a proposal to increase the bank's minimum capital requirement.

If a bank fails to achieve or maintain its minimum capital requirements, the OCC may, among other choices, issue a capital directive against the bank. If the OCC decides to issue a capital directive, it notifies the bank and solicits and carefully reviews the bank's views. If the OCC issues a capital directive, it sets forth in writing the reasons for issuing such an order. The capital directive becomes effective as soon as it is issued. The OCC may enforce a capital directive, or any plan the bank submits to comply with it, to the same extent as a C&D. However, unlike a C&D, a willful violation of or other failure to meet a capital directive is not itself grounds for receivership.

A capital directive, once issued, may require the bank to comply with any or all of the following:

☐ Achieve the minimum capital level applicable to it.

☐ Adhere to a preexisting plan to achieve the requisite capital level.

☐ Submit and adhere to a new capital plan.

☐ Take other actions, such as reducing assets or dividends, to restore the level of the bank's capital.

PROMPT CORRECTIVE ACTION DIRECTIVE

Under the prompt corrective action (PCA) legislation, the OCC and other banking agencies are required to establish five levels of capitalization for insured banks: well capitalized, adequately capitalized, undercapitalized, significantly undercapitalized, and critically under-capitalized. The legislation authorizes, and sometimes requires, the OCC to impose a wide range of requirements or restrictions on banks failing to maintain adequate capital, by issuing a PCA directive.

Unless there are immediate time constraints, the OCC notifies a bank in advance of its intention to impose discretionary PCA restrictions and gives the bank an opportunity to submit views on the matter. If the OCC decides to issue a PCA directive, the directive is enforceable in district court, and failure to submit or implement a capital restoration plan required in a PCA directive is grounds for receivership.

SAFETY AND SOUNDNESS ORDER

The OCC has the authority to require compliance with safety and soundness standards established by 12 CFR 30. These safety and soundness standards cover internal controls and information systems, internal audits, loan documentation, credit underwriting, interest rate exposure, asset growth, asset quality, earnings, compensation, information security, and residential mortgage lending.

The OCC may require the bank to submit a compliance plan that specifies how the bank will correct the deficiency. If the bank fails to submit or implement such a plan, the OCC may issue a safety and soundness order requiring the bank to take certain steps to correct the deficiencies. The order can be enforced in district court. A willful violation of a safety and soundness order is not itself grounds for receivership, but violation of substantial articles in a safety and soundness order can help establish the unsafe or unsound practices or condition that is an element of several receivership grounds.

OTHER ADMINISTRATIVE ACTIONS

CIVIL MONEY PENALTY

The OCC can assess such a penalty in various amounts depending on whether the act or omission was inadvertent, knowing, or reckless. The OCC's decision on the amount of the penalty is based on the consequences of the act or omission.

CONSERVATORSHIP AND RECEIVERSHIP

In severe cases, the OCC has the authority to place a bank into conservatorship or receivership. In a conservatorship, a conservator selected by the OCC manages the bank until the agency determines what action should be taken. In a receivership, the bank is closed immediately and handed over to the FDIC as receiver.

SECURITIES EXCHANGE ACT ACTIONS

The OCC may pursue other actions against banks that conduct securities activities subject to the Securities Exchange Act of 1934. Such securities activities—including acting as a broker-dealer, a government securities broker-dealer, a municipal securities dealer, or a transfer agent—may be performed by a bank or its operating subsidiary. The OCC has authority under the Securities Exchange Act to take action to redress violations of the federal securities laws by national banks and associated persons that the OCC supervises. Depending on the severity of the violation, the OCC may censure a bank that has engaged in improper activities. The OCC may deny or revoke a bank's registration for certain securities activities, thereby affecting the bank's ability to engage in such activities, or it may limit or suspend certain securities activities. The OCC may use these actions alone or in combination with other administrative remedies.

ACTIONS AGAINST INDIVIDUALS

The OCC has the authority to undertake certain administrative actions against individual bank directors or other IAPs. The agency may choose to take action if a director or other IAP

☐ Violates any law, rule or regulation, or outstanding agency order or agreement or condition imposed in writing.

☐ Engages in an unsafe or unsound banking practice or breaches a fiduciary duty.

The actions available to the OCC include a formal agreement, a C&D, a CMP, and a removal or prohibition action. These tools may require a director or other IAP to refrain from taking certain actions or they may require the director or other IAP to take certain affirmative actions (such as making restitution or correcting the problem).

CEASE-AND-DESIST ORDER

Occasionally, the OCC may request a director or other IAP who has engaged in a violation or an unsafe or unsound banking practice to enter into a consent order. The order might require the director or other IAP to take certain actions to correct the conditions that resulted from the violation or practice. It also might require the director or other IAP to reimburse the bank for losses resulting from the misconduct and might even restrict the director's or other IAP's activity with regard to the conduct at issue.

If the director or other IAP declines to enter into the order on a consensual basis and no settlement can be reached, the agency may issue a notice of charges against the individual. This notice seeks the formal issuance of a C&D and must set forth the specific charges against the director or other IAP. In addition, it must be based on one or more of the following:

☐ A violation of law, rule, or regulation.

☐ A violation of a condition imposed in writing by the agency in connection with the granting of an application.

☐ A violation of a formal agreement previously entered into.

☐ An unsafe or unsound banking practice.

The individual must file an answer to the charges contained in the notice, after which the matter proceeds to a formal administrative hearing in the same fashion as described previously with regard to administrative actions against banks.

PROHIBITION OR REMOVAL AND SUSPENSION

The OCC may initiate action to prohibit or remove a national bank director or other IAP from banking in cases in which particularly serious misconduct has occurred. In addition, the OCC may seek to prohibit a former director or other IAP. Prohibition and removal actions must be based on the following statutory elements, which address conduct, effect, and culpability:

☐ The individual must have engaged in or committed one or more of the following:

— A violation of law, rule, or regulation.

— A violation of a condition imposed in writing by the agency in connection with the granting of an application.

— A violation of an outstanding formal agreement or C&D.

— An unsafe or unsound banking practice.

— A breach of fiduciary duty.

□ The conduct described above must have resulted in

— A loss or potential loss or other damage to the bank,

— A financial gain or other benefit to the individual, or

— Prejudice to the interests of the depositors.

□ The individual's culpability for the conduct described must include either

— Personal dishonesty, or

— Willful or continuing disregard for the safety and soundness of the bank.

The hearing process for a prohibition or removal action is identical to a cease-and-desist hearing process. If adverse to the individual, the agency's decision may be appealed to a U.S. Court of Appeals.

Once in place, a prohibition or removal order prohibits the individual from participating, in any manner, in the conduct of the bank's affairs, participating in voting for a bank director, or serving or acting as a director, officer, employee, or other IAP. The removal or prohibition order applies to all federally insured depository institutions (including banks, thrifts, holding companies, credit unions, and farm credit institutions) and to all federal bank regulatory agencies.

Exceptions to the restrictions of a prohibition or removal order can be granted only if the affected individual receives the written consent of both the agency issuing the removal order and the agency supervising the financial institution with which the removed individual is seeking to become affiliated.

Once a removal action has been initiated, but before it is finalized, the OCC may issue a suspension order against the individual. This order temporarily removes the individual from the banking industry to the same extent as a final removal order. Such action is only taken, however, if the OCC determines that it is necessary to protect the national bank or its depositors. The suspended individual has the right to seek a stay of a suspension order from a federal district court within 10 days of the service of the suspension order. The suspension order is effective upon service by the OCC and remains in effect until the removal proceedings are completed, the OCC dismisses the charges, the agencies grant a written waiver, or the order is stayed by a court.

If a director or other IAP is indicted or charged with a felony involving dishonesty or breach of trust, or with a violation of the anti-money laundering statutes, the OCC also may suspend the individual after determining that the individual's continued service or affiliation with the bank may threaten the depositors' interests or may impair public confidence in the bank. The suspended individual may request an informal hearing before the agency to modify or terminate the suspension order. The suspension remains in effect until terminated by the OCC or until the criminal charges are resolved.

If a director or other IAP is convicted of any offense involving dishonesty, breach of trust, or money laundering, the individual is removed automatically from the banking industry. Under certain circumstances, the individual may petition the FDIC for permission to reenter banking.

CIVIL MONEY PENALTY

The OCC may assess a CMP of varying amounts against a director or other IAP for a violation of any law or regulation, temporary or permanent C&D, condition imposed in writing, or written agreement. In certain instances, the OCC may assess a CMP for unsafe and unsound banking practices that are reckless and for breaches of fiduciary duty.

When determining whether to bring a CMP action and the amount of the assessment, the OCC considers the following factors:

☐ The gravity of the violation.

☐ Any history of previous violations.

☐ Evidence of good faith.

☐ The individual's ability to pay.

☐ Other matters as justice may require.

The OCC's broad discretion to determine the amount of a CMP permits the agency to tailor the assessment to the facts of each case. For example, the OCC may assess an individual up to $7,500 a day for violations of any law or regulation, temporary or permanent C&D, condition imposed in writing, or written agreement. In certain circumstances, the OCC may assess a CMP of up to $37,500 a day for

☐ Any of the violations described above.

☐ Any unsafe and unsound banking practice engaged in recklessly.

☐ Any breach of fiduciary duty.

The OCC also has the authority to assess a CMP of $1,375,000 on a daily basis. These assessments can take place when the individual knowingly engaged in any violation, practice, or breach and, as a result of that conduct, knowingly or recklessly caused a substantial loss to the bank or knowingly or recklessly received a substantial gain or other benefit.

When determining the amount of a CMP assessment, the OCC takes into account the extent to which the bank has suffered a loss or the individual has received personal gain from the violation. In addition, the OCC will consider any mitigating factors, such as good faith, cooperation, or voluntary reimbursement for losses incurred by a bank. Conversely, the OCC may impose a more substantial penalty if an individual fails to cooperate with the OCC, fails to correct the violation, conceals the violation, or shows bad faith.

Before deciding whether to assess a CMP, the OCC gives the individual an opportunity to submit information about the alleged violation as well as the specific factors the OCC should consider when reviewing the case. After thoroughly reviewing the response and analyzing the case, the OCC will send the individual a "no action letter," a "supervisory letter," a "letter of reprimand," or a "notice of assessment." Supervisory letters and letters of reprimand state that no assessment will be imposed but advise that a future violation may result in a CMP assessment by the OCC.

If a CMP determination is made, the individual may request a formal agency hearing. The hearing and appeal procedures to review a CMP are the same as those for a C&D.

ACRONYMS

ALJ	administrative law judge
ALLL	allowance for loan and lease losses
BSA	Bank Secrecy Act
C&D	cease-and-desist order
CEO	chief executive officer
CFR	Code of Federal Regulations
CMP	civil money penalty
CRA	Community Reinvestment Act
FDIC	Federal Deposit Insurance Corporation
GAAP	generally accepted accounting principles
IAP	institution-affiliated party
IT	information technology
MOU	memorandum of understanding
NIM	net interest margin
OCC	Office of the Comptroller of the Currency
PCA	prompt corrective action
ROAA	return on average assets
ROE	return on equity
SEC	U.S. Securities and Exchange Commission
UBPR	Uniform Bank Performance Report
USC	U.S. Code

INDEX

H

Honorary directors, 5

I

Incentive compensation, 23–24, 33
Indemnification and insurance, 77, 92
Independent public accountant, 35–36
Informal enforcement actions, 95–96
Information security, 39, 88, 100
Information technology (IT), 13, 39, 107
Inside auditors, 35–38
Inside directors, 1–2, 3, 73
Insider activities, 36, 67–69, 74
Insider lending, 8, 38, 52, 53, 56, 67, 69, 84–86
Insider policies, 20, 67–69, 74–75
Insider trading, 20, 68, 89
Insider transactions, 69, 75, 81, 84–86
Institution-affiliated party (IAP), 91, 93, 101–104, 107
Interest rate risk, 9, 14, 31, 45, 58, 63
Internal audits, 39–42, 100
Internal controls, 1–2, 9, 34–37, 47, 64–66, 87
Interstate branching, 47
Investment activities, 61–62
Investment policy, 61–62

L

Large, complex banks, 16, 31, 38, 49, 51
Lending limits, 54–56, 69, 81–86
Limited-scope audit, 36–37
Liquidity risk, 31, 58–60, 67
Loan committee, 31, 44
Loan policy, 31, 52–53
Loan portfolio management, 44, 52–57
Loan review, 52–54
Loans to insiders, 8, 38, 52, 53, 56, 67, 69, 84–86

M

N

O

P

Procedures, 50
Prohibition, 102–104
Prompt corrective action (PCA), 10, 82, 95, 99, 107

R

Removal and suspension, 102–104
Report of Condition and Income (call report), 42, 82, 88
Reporting requirements, 36, 38, 69, 81, 88
Reputation risk, 15, 46, 65, 69
Risk categories, 13–15
Risk management, 10–17, 19, 21, 23–24, 31–32, 41–42, 50–51, 61–62, 65
Risk management committee, 29
Risk tolerance, 10–11

S

Safety and soundness order, 99–100
Safety and soundness plan, 96
Safety and soundness standards, 69, 87, 96, 99
Sarbanes-Oxley Act of 2002, 81–82
Securities, 89, 100–101
Securities and Exchange Commission (SEC), 18, 89, 107
Securities Exchange Act actions, 100
Securities laws, 70, 88–89
Securitized assets, 61
State laws, 18, 89
Statutory and regulatory liability, 77, 80–91
Strategic planning, 49–50
Strategic risk, 15, 50, 65
Supervision by risk, 12–17

T

Temporary cease and desist order, 95
Training and education programs, 2, 22, 68
Transactions with affiliates, 8, 25, 27, 67, 81, 86–87
Trust audit committee, 28
Trust committee, 32

U